P9-CBL-182

3 1611 00082 3242

DATE DUE

JUN 1 8 1999	
OCT 0 4 2004	

Measures of
Quality and
High Performance

Measures of Quality and High Performance

Simple Tools and Lessons
Learned From America's
Most Successful Corporations

Richard M. Hodgetts

GOVERNORS STATE UNIVERSITY
UNIVERSITY PARK
IL 60466

AMACOM

American Management Association

New York • Atlanta • Boston • Chicago • Kansas City • San Francisco • Washington, D.C.
Brussels • Mexico City • Tokyo • Toronto

HD 62.15 .H623 1998

Hodgetts, Richard M.

Measures of quality and high
performance

This book is available at a special
discount when ordered in bulk quantities.
For information, contact Special Sales Department,
AMACOM, a division of American Management Association,
1601 Broadway, New York, NY 10019.

This publication is designed to provide accurate and authoritative
information in regard to the subject matter covered. It is sold with the
understanding that the publisher is not engaged in rendering legal,
accounting, or other professional service. If legal advice or other expert
assistance is required, the services of a competent professional person
should be sought.

Library of Congress Cataloging-in-Publication Data

Hodgetts, Richard M.
    Measures of quality and high performance : simple tools and
lessons learned from America's most successful corporations /
Richard M. Hodgetts.
        p.   cm.
    Includes index.
    ISBN 0-8144-0377-8 (hardcover)
    1. Total quality management—Case studies.   2. Organizational
effectiveness—Case studies.   I. Title.
HD62.15.H623   1997
658.5'62—DC21   97-35583
                                                            CIP

© 1998 Richard M. Hodgetts
All rights reserved.
Printed in the United States of America.

This publication may not be reproduced,
stored in a retrieval system,
or transmitted in whole or in part,
in any form or by any means, electronic,
mechanical, photocopying, recording, or otherwise,
without the prior written permission of AMACOM,
a division of American Management Association,
1601 Broadway, New York, NY 10019.
Printing number

10   9   8   7   6   5   4   3   2   1

To
Ronald G. Greenwood
(1941–1995)

Teacher, researcher, author, friend

Contents

Acknowledgments

Many people provided me with support and assistance in writing this book. Anthony Vlamis, my acquisitions editor at AMACOM, was extremely influential in helping me redirect my initial ideas and focus my thinking. Don Bohl, editor of *Organizational Dynamics*, also provided me with useful suggestions and comments.

During the collection of data, I received a great deal of assistance from personnel at the companies I contacted. Many of them patiently and thoroughly explained the things their organization was doing and helped steer my efforts in a productive way. In particular, I am grateful to Carl Cooper, managing applications consultant at Motorola University, who spent a number of days with me, acquainting me with new tools and techniques that are being used by the company and securing a place for me in the company's quality briefing seminar. I am also thankful to Tom Land and Alan Barraclough, both formerly of Motorola's Training Department in Boynton Beach, Florida, who made phone calls and set up interviews with organizational personnel for me. I would also like to thank Patrick Mene, vice president of quality at the Ritz-Carlton in Atlanta, who sent me a wealth of information and took the time to talk with me on a number of different occasions. Robert Stempel, former president of the General Motors Corporation, helped clarify my thinking on the value and use of spider diagrams in benchmarking one's performance against world-class organizations. David Francesci of the Granite Rock Company carefully explained to me the company's use of quad graphics, and he sent me a film on the company's innovative operating procedures, all of which helped me better understand why the organization is a world-class performer. I would also like to thank Bob Wainwright of Wainwright Industries for his continued support of my efforts. Thanks also goes to the individuals who helped me obtain permission to use materials from their organizations and who checked my facts to ensure that they were both correct and current. Among others, these include Susan Grove (AT&T Consumer Markets Division), Chuck Roberts (Ames Rubber), Joyce Lehman (Armstrong Building Products), Leslie Antos (Corning Telecommunications Products), Dorothy Faquin (FedEx), Robert Hess (GE Plastics), Elizabeth Galbraith Miller (GTE Directories), Steve Hoisington (IBM), Peggy Dellinger (Lucent Technologies), Elaine Casey (Motorola), and Sam Malone (Xerox). Finally, I would like to thank the companies that provided me information on a wide variety of their quality and measurement tools and techniques. In alphabetical order, they include:

Ames Rubber Corporation
Andersen Windows
Armstrong Building Products Operations
AT&T Consumer Communications Services
AT&T Network Systems Group
AT&T Universal Card Services
Corning Telecommunications Products Division
Eastman Chemical Company
Federal Express Corporation
General Electric Plastics America
Granite Rock Company
GTE Directories Corporation
IBM
Lucent Technologies
Marlow Industries
Milliken & Company
Motorola Corporation
Texas Instruments Defense Systems & Electronics Group
Ritz-Carlton Hotel Company
Solectron Company
Wainwright Industries Inc.
Xerox Corporation's Business Products & Systems
Zytec Corporation

Finally, I would like to thank my colleagues at Florida International University (FIU) and at other academic institutions who provided me with materials, read parts of this manuscript and offered substantive comments, and encouraged me in this effort: Hal Wyman, former dean of the College of Business at FIU; Gary Dessler, chairman of the Department of Management and International Business at FIU; Ellie Browner, director of the Center for Management Development at FIU; Cindy Elliott, head of Distance Learning, FIU; Crystal Duxbury, vice president of human resources, and Allan Sutherland, chief financial officer, both of the Henry Lee Company; John Goebel, dean of the College of Business at the University of Nebraska—Lincoln (UNL); Fred Luthans, UNL; Sang Lee, UNL; Jane Gibson and Charles Blackwell, Nova Southeastern University; Alan Rugman, University of Toronto; and Rosabeth Moss Kanter, Harvard University.

Measures of Quality and High Performance

Introduction

When I first formulated the idea for writing this book, I did so with a working title that I believed would cleverly summarize the contents: *Total Quality Management: What's Hot, What's Not.* My objective was first to choose those companies that had been nationally recognized as offering the highest-quality goods and services. These would be the Baldrige award winners, beginning with the first group of winners—Motorola, Westinghouse Electric's Commercial Nuclear Fuel Division, and Globe Metallurgical—and continuing on to the most recent. In each case, I intended to find out the tools and techniques that the company used at the time it won the Malcolm Baldrige Award and then to update the story by finding out which of these approaches it no longer used and what new ones had emerged and were now highly popular in the company.

My first set of interviews took place at Motorola, where I quickly learned that, in the battle to maintain high quality and performance, the company was still doing what it had done in the past—but had added some new approaches as well. This pattern was reinforced by all of the other Baldrige winners I contacted, making me realize that the battle for quality and high performance is not one of replacing old tools with new ones but of developing *supplemental* approaches and techniques that can take the organization to ever higher levels. This caused me to rethink my approach and to focus on gaining a clearer picture of how successful companies manage to become world-class competitors. In the process, I began to realize that in measuring their quality and performance and using these data to improve operations, these companies were employing a host of simple, yet extremely effective tools and techniques. Moreover, after gathering the data for the first chapter and carefully reviewing the information, I also realized that there were lessons that these organizations had learned and that served to focus and direct their efforts. In turn, this provided me with the framework for identifying and discussing both operational steps and lessons to be derived from these activities.

As a result, I changed my approach to the book. Instead of focusing on "what was hot and what was not," I changed the orientation and began looking at how high-performing companies (most of which were Baldrige winners) go about measuring quality and then taking the necessary steps to both improve output and increase competitiveness. In the process, I also turned each chapter into a self-learning exercise that allows the reader to apply what he or she has learned by drawing on the very lessons I discovered in researching the chapter.

What I Learned

There were three things I learned in gathering, analyzing, and writing this book. These relate to environmental and operational considerations, new developments in improving quality and measuring performance, and useful lessons derived from the information.

First, while I began my efforts by focusing on finding new tools and techniques, I soon realized that much of what was being communicated to me by these companies related to what I now call "pre-tool" considerations. These companies could not formulate a strategy for developing a highly competitive organization until they had first addressed two other issues: (1) their view of the world in which they were competing; and (2) the type of organizational interrelationships and esprit de corps they had to create in order to be successful. Simply put, the organizations had to examine their mind-sets and then create (or re-create) the culture that would be needed for success. The specific considerations within each of these areas are addressed in Chapters 1 and 2.

The second thing I learned is that while all of these companies were trying to do things better—as opposed to doing new things—there were indeed a number of new developments that were proving extremely helpful to them in measuring quality and high performance and taking the needed follow-up steps. For example, Xerox's customer satisfaction survey instrument is highly useful in pinpointing buyer concerns and helping the organization identify ways in which it can be more effective. The same is true for Granite Rock's customer feedback and supplier evaluation surveys, which allow the company to develop a "quad graph" and to determine steps for improving performance and winning new customers. Similarly, Armstrong Building Products Operations' approach to market segmentation has allowed it to both identify and analyze high-leverage and critical improvement issues. Another new development is Motorola's Quality System Review, which is now being used companywide to measure a wide variety of activities, from new product technology to supplier performance to equipment and systems control to customer satisfaction. These are only a handful of the new concepts that are being used, but they all point to the fact that successful companies must develop innovative tools and techniques if they hope to stay ahead of the competition.

The third thing I learned is that there is a host of simple lessons that these companies use to maintain their competitiveness. In one way or another, each employs these lessons. In all, twenty lessons have been culled from my research. In every chapter of this book I have identified and described two or three lessons that are employed in addressing the main issues under discussion. The first six, in Chapters 1 and 2, focus on mind-sets and culture and are presented as lessons that enterprises "ought" to follow. Lessons 7 through 20 are drawn from the operational chapters and are presented as "directives" to be implemented. These twenty lessons, presented in the order in which they appear in the book, are these:

Mind-Sets and Cultural Lessons

Lesson 1: Old myths have to be replaced by new truths.
Lesson 2: Customer value added is the name of the game.
Lesson 3: Training is the paradigm buster.
Lesson 4: Cultural change has to begin with a careful formulation of strategic intent.
Lesson 5: Cultural change will be sustained only if there are adequate support mechanisms.

Lesson 6: Cultural changes have to be validated through measurement.

Operational Lessons

Lesson 1: Identify the key factors that are critical for superior customer satisfaction.

Lesson 2: Carefully craft forms of feedback for determining customer satisfaction.

Lesson 3: Determine the status of the results, and take any necessary action for correcting errors and improving customer satisfaction.

Lesson 4: Make training and development mandatory and ongoing.

Lesson 5: Develop specific tools that work for the organization.

Lesson 6: Review and measure the value of the training tools.

Lesson 7: Decide what should be tracked.

Lesson 8: Systematically gather and evaluate these data.

Lesson 9: Carefully and thoroughly assess personnel performance.

Lesson 10: Create a process for fully developing the potential of each individual.

Lesson 11: Develop a system for recognizing all outstanding performance.

Lesson 12: Create a reward program that is designed especially for your organization.

Lesson 13: Look for ways to innovate the current work processes and procedures.

Lesson 14: Develop an effective benchmarking and continuous improvement system that relies on new-age thinking.

How This Book Will Help You

There are a number of ways in which this book will help you. Primarily, it will make you aware of how world-class organizations measure quality and achieve high performance, thus providing you guidelines for increasing your own competitiveness. In particular, this book will help you do the following:

- ► Evaluate your organization's mind-set regarding operational beliefs, and begin separating myth from fact.
- ► Understand why a customer-added-value strategy is now becoming the name of the game.
- ► Know how to link organizational culture and strategic intent, and use this knowledge for creating changes that are productive and profitable.
- ► Be able to develop support mechanisms for sustaining cultural change.
- ► Know how to identify the key factors that are critical for customer satisfaction, and develop specific, measurable targets for assessing progress in this area.
- ► Be able to create training tools that are effective and efficient, and know how to review and measure the value of these tools on an ongoing basis.
- ► Know how to track results in key operating areas by systematically identifying output measures, gathering these data, and then evaluating the information and making informed follow-on decisions.
- ► Develop organization-specific performance assessment tools that focus heavily on associate development and help ensure that the full potential of all employees is developed.
- ► Create recognition and reward programs that motivate employees to pursue challenging, profitable objectives, and sustain this effort for the indefinite future.

Another way in which this book will help you is by familiarizing you with some of the latest tools and techniques that are being used to increase organizational performance. In addition to those already mentioned, others include the strategic use of customer value added, bottom-up employee performance evaluations, the linking of technology and customer requirements, and the use of spiderweb diagrams to plot performance and compare it to that of the competition or benchmark it against world-class organizations.

Still another way this book will help you is by providing the opportunity to apply what you are learning to your own organization. At the end of each chapter there is a section titled "Examining Your Own Organizational Performance," which has a number of assignments that are specifically designed to help you and your management team use what you have learned in the chapter.

My overriding goal in writing this book has been to answer this question: What do managers need to know in order to measure quality and performance and thus run their organizations as efficiently and effectively as do world-class enterprises? The answers at which I arrived showed me that every enterprise can apply the same simple, practical principles that are being followed by these successful organizations. It's all a matter of finding out what needs to be done—and then committing yourself and your personnel to doing it!

Part I

Fundamental Considerations of High-Performance Companies

High-performing companies are able to achieve their objectives and outpace the competition because they have created the right conditions for their success. In doing so, their initial focus is *not* on measuring operating results such as error rates, cycle time, or inventory control. Rather, it is on careful consideration of the environment in which they are operating and identification of the changes that will have to be created if they are to be successful in the future. These considerations can be summarized in two words: mind-sets and culture.

A *mind-set* is an organization's view of its operating world. As such, it guides decision making and helps senior executives formulate and implement strategy. So far, there is nothing new about this; companies employ the process every day. However, the most competitive businesses do one thing before they employ the information in their mind-set—they examine and evaluate its accuracy. Are they proceeding on the basis of facts or of suppositions, beliefs, hunches, and intuitive feelings that represent collective and erroneous information? In a way, successful companies are strong adherents of the message that Will Rogers, the world-renowned humorist, shared with his audience one day after visiting Herbert Hoover at the White

House. When he left the meeting and the waiting reporters asked about his conversation with the president, Rogers remarked, "What worries me ain't the things he doesn't know, but what he knows that just ain't so!" Rogers obviously felt that Hoover had some erroneous mind-sets that were causing him to make decisions that were hurting the economy. This same analogy holds true for many companies that proceed on the basis of what might be called "misinformation." In dealing with this problem, highly competitive organizations do three things. First, they carefully review their operating data and competitive analyses and replace old myths with new truths. For example, many businesses believe that quality may be an admirable objective but that there is a feasibility range for improvements and quality should not be increased beyond this point; if the company goes beyond that point, it will find that quality efforts do not pay off. However, world-class companies such as Motorola argue just the opposite, holding that a company never reaches the point of diminishing return—and that those who disagree with this statement are clinging to old myths. Given Motorola's performance and international reputation, it seems likely that its beliefs regarding the need for increasing quality have more substance than critics might want to acknowledge.

Unfortunately, mind-sets are not easily changed. And this is where training enters the picture, for it is one of the great paradigm busters. With effective training, employees can be taught how to do things that they intuitively believed were not possible. Companies such as Federal Express (FedEx), the Ritz-Carlton, Wainwright Industries, and Xerox provide goods or services that not just meet but exceed the demanding expectations of their customers! It can be done—but only if the personnel are effectively trained in three ways: how to do it, how to do it right, and how to do it right every time.

Do it right every time? This is an objective that every organization embraces. However, the world-class companies studied in this book go one step beyond setting demanding goals. They also work on changing their cultures so that the beliefs, attitudes, values, and expectations of the personnel are in sync with the strategy of the enterprise. Motorola has three basic beliefs that it shares with everyone who attends one of its quality briefings and that explain both why and how cultural change can be implemented: (1) when culture and strategy clash, invariably culture wins out; (2) if the organizational culture does not embrace initiatives related to change, overall change efforts will fail; and (3) what gets measured gets done. Simply put, you can't change the organization's strategy without first changing the culture. And if you want people to change, you have to measure what they are doing and reward it.

The two chapters in this part of the book address the fundamental considerations that create the environment for high-performance organizations. In addition to comparing old myths and new truths, Chapter 1 explains why customer added value is now the name of the game in world-class organizations and why the role that training plays in helping bring about this new emphasis is paramount. The chapter also describes how these successful companies have managed to change their mind-sets and remain on the cutting edge in areas such as quality of output, employee performance, and customer needs. In many cases these companies have become industry leaders because what competitors viewed as impossible they saw as future opportunities.

The second chapter in this part looks at the way highly successful businesses evaluate their cultures and make the necessary changes. In doing so, they take three critical steps. First, they develop a future view of their competitive world. Second, they create what are called "support mechanisms" that help bring about cultural change. Third, they validate these changes through measurement and take appropriate action on the basis of the results. In this way, they continue to close the loop between the culture they want to create and the one they have.

Chapter 1

Face Facts: It's a Whole New Ball Game

Most world-class companies did not wake up one morning and decide that they wanted to pursue higher-quality initiatives. In many cases they were *forced* to change because they were non-competitive and, in some instances cases, facing financial or marketing crises. A number of companies fit into this category, including Baldrige-Award-winning operations such as Globe Metallurgical, Motorola, Wainwright Industries, Xerox, and Zytec.

Sometimes, fortunately, the wake-up call came early. A good example is offered by Bob Galvin, Motorola's CEO when it won the Baldrige Award. Galvin likes to tell the story about how he and a group of senior executives were reviewing company progress one day and discussing ways the company could become even more competitive. Suddenly one of the most respected members of the marketing group interrupted and said, "I know that we are trying very hard to be the best company we can, but quite frankly—quality stinks!' This statement came as a surprise to the rest of the executives, but given the man's reputation and tenure with Motorola, they began discussing the statement, then started investigating performance, and soon concluded that there was indeed a lot more they had to do to improve quality. It took the statement "quality stinks" to wake them up to the fact that their approach to doing business was not as good as they thought. Since that time, of course, Motorola has introduced a wide variety of quality-related tools and approaches throughout its organization, including six sigma, reduced cycle time, and the development of hundreds of new technical and management development courses. In the process, the company, like other world-class organizations, has discovered that the old way of doing things is no longer competitive. Simply put: Today, it's a whole new ballgame.

This opening chapter contains three central ideas that will be developed in reinforcing this statement. These are best thought of as lessons that America's most competitive businesses learned that helped them become world-class operations. They include:

1. *New truths are now replacing old myths.* A lot of what people "know" regarding quality, cost, and effective operations is just not true. As a result, their companies are not as competitive as they should be because they are using last year's information to compete in tomorrow's markets.

2. *Customer added value is now the name of the game.* Companies that don't know what their customer wants and how they can improve the product or service so that they can add more value without increasing price are at a distinct disadvantage.

3. *Training is the great paradigm buster.* Paradigms are mindsets that influence the way we think. The only way to learn new ways of thinking is to reject old paradigms and replace them with more accurate ones. This is where training comes into the picture. Of course, sometimes training programs, at best, are only moderately effective because they are geared to the wrong group or do not provide the information and experience that the participants need. When they are properly designed and implemented, however, they can help organizations change their old ways of thinking and become more competitive.

The following section examines how the companies studied in this book have used these three lessons to compete in today's ballgame. After you have finished reading these three lessons, the final section of the chapter provides the opportunity to apply them to your own enterprise.

Lesson 1: Old Myths Have to Be Replaced by New Truths

Over the past decade it has become obvious that many of the old organizational beliefs regarding quality, cost, and the nature of operations have been based on erroneous or incomplete information. Companies that have won the Baldrige, in particular, have carefully examined and refuted many of these myths and replaced them with new truths that are based on information gathered in the workplace and verified through analysis and experimentation. Table 1-1 provides a brief comparison of some of these myths and truths. In most cases, this new thinking can be explained in terms of costs, beliefs, and/or attitudes.

Costs And Quality Are Inversely Related

One of the most popular myths is that quality costs a great deal of money; therefore, organizations have to balance a concern for cost with a desire for quality by striking a balance between the two. The illustration in Figure 1-1 provides an example of this thinking. A close look at the figure shows that as failure rates are driven down (and quality rises), the costs associated with this progress rise, slowly at first but then ever more rapidly. If the organization were to increase quality to the point where failures were zero (or highly negligible), the cost would be astronomical, so the enterprise must be willing to determine an acceptable error rate and be content with this level of quality. As shown in Figure 1-1, this point occurs where there is the best cost/benefit tradeoff between errors and expenditures.

More recent research shows that Figure 1-1 does not provide an accurate explanation of the quality/cost relationship. In fact, as quality is driven up, overall expenses tend to go down. This idea is represented in Figure 1-2, which illustrates the costs associated with varying degrees of "sigma." *Sigma* is a measure of defects per unit as a percentage of the total number of opportunities for defects per unit. The higher the sigma, the lower the

(Text continues on page 16.)

Table 1-1. The emergence of new beliefs.

Old Myth	New Truth
Quality is the responsibility of the people in the quality control department.	Quality is everyone's job.
Training is costly.	Training does not cost; it saves.
New quality programs have high initial costs.	The best quality programs do not have upfront costs.
Better quality will cost the company a lot of money.	As quality goes up, costs come down.
The measurement of data should be kept to a minimum.	An organization cannot have too much relevant data on hand.
It is human to make mistakes.	Perfection—total customer satisfaction—is a standard that should be vigorously pursued.
Some defects are major and should be addressed, but many are minor and can be ignored.	No defects are acceptable, regardless of whether they are major or minor.
Quality improvements are made in small, continuous steps.	In improving quality, both small and large improvements are necessary.
Quality improvement takes time.	Quality does not take time; it saves time.
Haste makes waste.	Thoughtful speed improves quality.
Quality programs are best oriented toward areas such as products and manufacturing.	Quality is important in all areas, including administration and service.
After a company makes a number of quality improvements, customers are no longer able to see additional improvements.	Customers are able to see all improvements, including those in price, delivery, and performance.
Good ideas can be found throughout the organization.	Good ideas can be found everywhere, including in the operations of competitors and in organizations that provide similar goods and services.
Suppliers need to be price competitive.	Suppliers need to be quality competitive.

Source: Motorola Corporation, 1996.

Figure 1-1. The old assumption regarding the relationship between cost and quality.

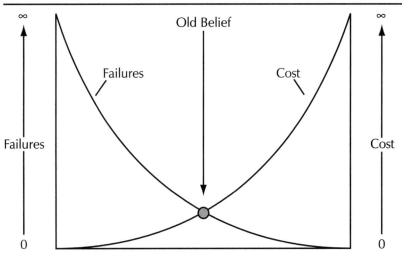

Source: Motorola quality briefing, 1996.

Figure 1-2. The new assumptions regarding the relationship between cost and quality.

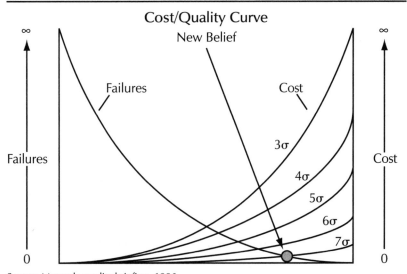

Source: Motorola quality briefing, 1996.

error rate. As related to Figure 1-2, these rates are the following:

3 sigma	66,810 errors per million
4 sigma	6,210 errors per million
5 sigma	233 errors per million
6 sigma	3.4 errors per million
7 sigma	virtually no errors per million

By increasing quality, an organization actually drives *down* its costs. There are a number of reasons for this result. One is that the costs associated with correcting mistakes are eliminated since everything is done right the first time (or much sooner than previously), thus saving the company the expenses associated with reworking. A second reason is that the organization begins building a reputation as a highly reliable supplier or manufacturer and thus attracts more business. This, in turn, helps the company spread its fixed costs among more buyers and drives down costs even more. So far from costing money, in most cases increased quality more than pays for itself and proves to be a critical driver in ensuring that the enterprise is both cost effective and profitable.

Beliefs Are Changing

Beliefs are convictions and opinions that influence behavior. As shown in Table 1-1, a number of quality-related beliefs that are common among world-class organizations help the enterprises plan and implement their efforts. One is the belief that quality is everyone's job. Instead of having a quality control department that is responsible for this activity, they delegate this responsibility to the department and unit level and empower the personnel in these areas to take whatever steps are needed to ensure quality.

A second belief is that quality comes in all sizes—big and small. This thinking is a change from what was accepted a few years ago when the Japanese popularized the concept of *kaizen*, or continuous improvement (CI) and encouraged everyone in the firm to strive for small, steady improvements in their work output. It has become clear that incremental CI can be self-defeating because it discourages innovation and rethinking of the big picture. The new thinking adopted by Xerox holds that if incremental CI is not generating much of an increase in quality, attention should be directed toward the overall design of the way in which the product is being made or the service delivered for the purpose of determining if a new approach can spark a more innovative route to increasing quality.

A third new belief is that reducing the time it takes to do things actually increases quality. The logic behind this statement is found in the cliché "If you can't do it any better, do it faster." While this belief can be self-defeating, since it is possible that the increased speed will result in employees spending more time correcting mistakes than they save by moving faster, highly competitive companies have been able to gain a time advantage while sidestepping the error problems, typically by carefully designing the job, giving the personnel thorough training, and getting feedback on results so that common mistakes are eliminated. The essence of this belief is that by reducing cycle time for a job, the company also reduces the time opportunity for the individual to make mistakes.

A fourth belief underlying new quality thinking is that these ideas can be used everywhere in the organization, from manufacturing to services to administration, as well as with outside groups, such as suppliers and vendors. These beliefs serve as a basis for linking the enterprise and some of its key external constituencies, thus providing the organization an opportunity to develop quality-related objectives and a blueprint for getting everyone involved in both planning and organizing the necessary effort.

Attitudes Are Also Changing

Attitudes are feelings that people have toward other people and things. In Table 1-1 I included two important attitudes that world-class companies hold regarding quality. The first is that the old adage "to err is human" is no longer acceptable. These companies believe that a goal of zero errors is doable, and they pursue this goal relentlessly. The second, and related, attitude is that a "no defects" policy relates to both major *and* minor problems. The belief that major mistakes must be avoided at all costs but minor ones can be allowed because they do not generate a great deal of expense is rejected under the new thinking.

These new attitudes may be viewed as utopian. There will always be errors, and when they occur it is important to address the major ones first in order to contain the overall damage. However, world-class companies have the attitude that if a company starts feeling that some errors are acceptable, it is going to end up losing profit and market share to those companies that are adamant in their pursuit of zero defects and that refuse to compromise. To this extent, then, the new thinking involves a mind game in which common logic (there will always be errors) is overridden by boundless determination (errors are simply unacceptable).

Lesson 2: Customer Value Added Is the Name of the Game

In addition to reformulating their thinking and rejecting old myths, world-class companies have helped change the ballgame in another critical way: They have developed systems for adding customer value. Depending on the company, of course, the process will vary. In this section we look at two ways in which customer value added (CVA) has been used to focus quality direction. The first describes the approach employed by Lucent Technologies when it was part of AT&T just a few years ago. The second is the approach currently used by Motorola.

Perceived Value Is Critical

Lucent Technologies' customer-value-added philosophy flowed from the belief that long-term profit is a result of revenue streams generated by customers who are continuously satisfied with the service they are receiving and who are unwilling to take their business to anyone else. Working from this perceptual system, Lucent defined CVA as:

Providing products and services to customers that are a greater value than they could expect from purchases from competitive companies in similar markets.

In providing CVA to its customers, Lucent also developed a series of premises that provided the foundation for its quality-driven strategy. Four of the key ones include:

1. People buy on perceived value.
2. Value is a function of quality relative to price.
3. Quality includes all nonprice attributes.
4. Quality, price, and value are all relative measures.

Research by Lucent revealed some interesting linkages among perception, quality, price, and profit. For example, the company found that customers who saw themselves as receiving higher quality were also more willing to pay higher prices. So *perceived* superior quality earned price premiums. In addition, and as noted in Table 1-1, higher quality does not always mean higher costs. In fact, Lucent found that as quality increased, costs tended to decline and then slowly increased. Overall, the cost of the increased quality remained significantly less than the price paid by the customer. Result: *Superior quality drives both profitability and market share.*

In order to employ CVA as a strategy, Lucent formulated consumer-value-added strategic goals and developed a system for plotting progress toward these targets. The organization's five CVA strategic goals included:

1. Strengthen the company's position as a customer-focused, market-driven business.
2. Formulate a business strategy based on the customer's set of facts and priorities.
3. Grow the business by generating value for the customer.
4. Consider competitor strengths and weaknesses in formulating business strategy.
5. Use CVA as an early warning system to capture shifts in customer priorities and preferences.

The company pursued these objectives by first identifying price satisfaction and customer satisfaction scores for both itself and its competitors. It then determined those steps that had to be taken in order to distance itself from the competition and reach its own targeted position. The value map in Figure 1-3 provides an example. On this value map Lucent's Transmission Systems group has a quality satisfaction score of 7.1 and a price satisfaction score of 7.7. These are both better than its competitor's scores, which are 7.1 and 6.2, respectively. However, Lucent's objectives for quality and price satisfaction scores are 9.0 and 8.5, so the Transmission Systems group needs to continue its improvement efforts. This will be done by identifying steps it can take to close the perceived gap between its current scores and its goals and by determining steps it can take to introduce countermeasures vis-à-vis the competition. Once these are done, Lucent will then implement the needed deployment activities and again measure results—and this process will go on continu-

Figure 1-3. Lucent Technologies' strategic use of CVA: transmission systems example.

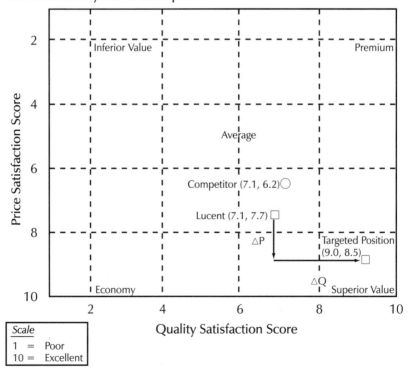

Source: Lucent Technologies.

ally, as the company strives to reach and maintain its targeted position.

In Lucent's case CVA is a function of price and quality satisfaction as determined by customer perception. So whether or not the individual receives a better price or higher quality service from a competitor is not the primary issue. It is how the person perceives what he or she is receiving that counts. In many cases CVA has been generated in a less subjective way. Motorola provides a good example.

Faster Can Also Be Better

Motorola focuses on customer value in a number of ways. One is by reducing the time needed to produce and deliver its products. Since Motorola pagers and cellular phones have world-class quality built into them, the company focuses on getting them to market faster. In the case of pagers, for example, the company has reduced cycle time from fifty-six days to less than one hour! It has done this by implementing a number of important steps.

Types of Performance

One step has been to determine how long it takes to produce a product and then compare this time to more desirable levels. The company does this by looking at three types of performance: baseline, entitlement, and strategic best. *Baseline* is a quantitative description of the standard against which progress is to be measured, such as fifty-six days to produce a pager. *Entitlement* is the best level of performance that the company can expect, given its current investment in plant, equipment, software, designs, processes, and people. When Motorola first began studying cycle time, it found that it was "entitled" to 200 to 300 percent more than its current baseline performance. In manufacturing operations, for example, entitlement was two and one-half times the time in which any product was being manufactured, when all queues and nonprocess-related wait time were eliminated. In the case of administrative office work, the company found that entitlement was one-thirtieth of the current processing time! *Strategic best* is the highest competitive performance and typically requires the investment of additional resources and corrective action that further reduce waste and increase efficiency.

When Motorola made a comparison of these three levels, it found that baseline performance distributions are typically characterized by below-performance potential and long cycle times. Entitlement distributions are significantly better and have more predictable results and shorter cycle time. And strategic best distributions represent world-class performance and have very short cycle times. The company's objective has been to move from baseline to entitlement performance and then to add additional resources to reach strategic best. Two good examples of how this has been done are its order write-ups and its handling of new product development cycles.

Order Write-Ups

In the past, it was typical for Motorola to give customers a delivery date and then measure performance against this date. Today the company has changed to customer-requested delivery dates, which allows the buyer to determine when the product is to be delivered. Any failure to meet this customer-set date is regarded as a "delinquency." Because of this new approach, Motorola has been forced to shorten its cycle time. It has done this by breaking down cycle time into its basic elements, beginning with the write-up of the order and ending with the shipment of the product. As noted in Figure 1-4, it used to take 8.1 days to write up an order and submit it to the area office. Today this has been reduced to .2 days, thanks to the use of faxes, priority mail, and other rapid-speed means of communication. At the same time, the company changed its sales quota system so that salespeople did not hang on to orders until the last minute but submitted them as quickly as possible.

The company has also focused attention on the way it processed orders. It used to take almost two weeks for employees to handle an order, partly because nothing was done until all the paperwork was received. This process was changed so that work

Figure 1-4. Cycle time reduction in the communications sector (in days).

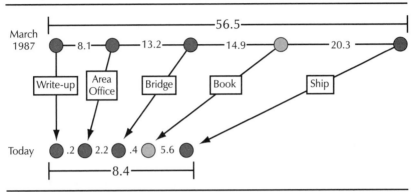

Source: Motorola, 1996.

now begins the moment an order is received, no matter what form it takes.

Another reason for processing delays was that employees formerly took steps in sequential order. First, they entered information in the computer system; then they conducted a credit check, a process that often took two to four days and sometimes as long as a month. Moreover, no one was ever turned down for credit; if there was a problem, the company simply went back to the customer for more information. To speed up the process, Motorola has set up an automatic approval system so that, in most cases, credit requests of $5,000 or less are automatically approved.

Motorola has also simplified its computerized order entry and processing program, put in fewer screens, and made the process virtually foolproof. As a result, if an employee makes an error in entering information or omits critical data, the computer will signal the operator and not allow the individual to proceed to the next screen. This system ensures accuracy and reduces the time needed to enter orders. Because of these steps, the average time for processing orders has been reduced to 2.2 days.

Motorola also looked into how to book orders into the factory for fabrication and then shipment. In the first case, the number of days has dropped from 14.9 to .4, and in the second from 20.3 to 5.6. In both areas the company continues to monitor closely the time needed to carry out the functions, and it continually looks for ways of shortening the process. For example, the company has redesigned some products so that they have fewer parts and are easier to assemble. As a result, since 1993 Motorola has been able to cut order cycle time in the communications sector by more than 16 percent.

New Product Development Cycles

Another way in which Motorola has used cycle time is to shorten new product development. This has been done through the use of a "contract book" process. For every new product, the company creates a contract book that contains all of the features and requirements necessary to ensure total customer satisfaction. In the case of popular consumer products such as pagers and portable two-way radios, much of this information is obtained from focus groups and blind market surveys; in the case of specialized products designed for a single customer or small groups, the marketing and engineering people work closely with buyers to put together the contract book.

When the process is completed, all departments that provide support for the product review what they are going to do. At this point they also agree on the specific deliverables they will provide, the ways in which each deliverable will be measured, and the date on which (or by which) this will be done. They then sign off on the contract, which becomes the final guide in ensuring total customer satisfaction.

One of the primary benefits of the contract book is that it freezes product requirements and specifications. Changes may be made at a later date, but the basic plan remains the same, and all departments allocate their resources to conform to it. This approach helps reduce cycle time in all three phases of new product development: concept, design, and manufacturing. All three phases also take much less time when a contract book is used. In fact, before the contract-book approach was employed, it took two to six years to introduce a new portable product. Today, in some areas such as mobile products, cycle time has been cut to under six months.

Lesson 3: Training Is the Paradigm-Buster

The first step in dealing with the quality paradigm is to accept its existence. The second step is to realize that those companies that offer better quality and value to the customer will dominate their markets and have higher returns on investment than the competition. The third step is to train personnel to deal with their new environment by doing things at least as well as the competition—and, one hopes, a great deal better. There are a variety of ways in which this is done by world-class organizations. One of the best examples is provided by Motorola, which offers hundreds of courses to personnel at all levels of the hierarchy, from the factory floor to the executive suite.

Early Learning Experiences Are Important

The Motorola Training and Education Center, or Motorola University (MU for short), was started in 1980. Over the past two decades it has changed both its focus and its strategy as to how to carry out its tasks. In particular, the group learned that many of its initial ideas regarding training and education, especially in the manufacturing area, were incorrect or only partly true. As a result, MU ended up changing its education paradigm.

At first the training and education center decided that its charter would be not so much to educate people as to be an agent of change. Emphasis would be given to training workers and redefining jobs. So MU started out by looking at current manufacturing jobs and trying to anticipate what these jobs would look like in the future. On the basis of its findings, it developed curricula and training programs. For example, to meet the goal of increasing output quality, it developed a five-part curriculum. The first part addressed statistical process control, including such well-known tools as checksheets, histograms, Pareto analysis, cause-and-effect analysis, flow charts, scatter diagrams, and control charts. The second part focused on basic industrial problem solving. The third trained participants in effective ways of presenting conceptual material. The fourth taught individuals to run effective meetings, and the fifth trained them to define objectives, put these in writing, and measure progress toward them.

On paper, the new program looked ideal, but it did *not* work. One reason was that the people who would have benefited from these courses did not sign up for them. Many of these individuals were accustomed to learning new tools and techniques on the job, not in a classroom setting, so they did not see the benefits of the new curriculum. Moreover, many of them had worked for Motorola from the time they finished high school or college, and they knew that after they reached the ten-year mark the company would never terminate them except for poor performance or dishonesty. They did not see a reason to upgrade their skills through formal study, since this was unlikely to have any effect on their employment. A second reason for the failure of the new curriculum was that the senior-level staff did not actively participate. They were briefed on the new quality programs that were being offered, but they did not openly embrace the courses by attending them or talking to the lower-level personnel about what was being taught and how the people were using these new ideas. As a result, many trainees seldom applied what they had been taught at MU. They simply went about their jobs as usual.

A few years after the MU training efforts began, Motorola decided to find out how well these programs were paying off. It had experts from two universities come in, gather data, and evaluate the results. They found that return on the training investment dollar varied sharply among three groups:

1. In those few plants where the workforce took the entire curriculum of quality tools and process skills and applied them on the job and senior management reinforced these efforts, the company achieved a $33 return for every $1 spent, including the wages paid to participants while they were in class.

2. In those plants where the participants made use of the quality tools or the process skills but not both and were then reinforced for what they were doing, the company broke even on its investment.

3. In those plants where all or part of the curriculum was taught but there was no reinforcement on the part of management through follow-up meetings and a genuine emphasis on quality, the company earned a negative return on its investment.

The lesson was clear: Change not only had to be driven from the top; it had to *begin* at the top. So MU went back to the drawing board and decided to upgrade the status, rewards, and recruiting of manufacturing personnel. It also created a new two-week program of courses designed to prepare the workers for manufacturing jobs in the upcoming decade. However, the group *again* failed to realize that senior managers would not sign up for these courses. These managers simply delegated them to lower-level personnel. This is when the training group's advisory board, headed by the chief executive officer, changed the approach and began "inviting" top managers (including board members) to come to the training. At the same time, the courses began to center on some of the concepts that would eventually make Motorola a world-class organization in manufacturing: empowerment, cycle time, and the creation of a boundaryless organization in which all departments fully cooperated with each other. In addition, a special training and education development seminar was created for senior management. (Each year the seminar has a central theme, such as global competition, cycle-time management, or new product development.) These efforts were beginning to get top management more actively involved in the training effort. At last, the company believed, it would be easier to drive training down the line. Once again, however, their efforts were stymied—this time because the company had failed to carefully examine the educational level of the workforce.

In the mid-1980s Motorola had decided to open its new cellular manufacturing facility in the United States rather than take it offshore. The company felt that its workforce should be able to compete with any in the world, so why not keep the work at home? At the new manufacturing facility outside Chicago, the workforce knew radio technology and, given the similarities, the company felt confident that these workers could make the bridge to cellular. The group had increased quality tenfold in the first five years of training and was well on its way to repeating that achievement. One way in which this was to be done was by empowering the workers so that they could take much more responsibility than previously, including carrying out quality control and flexible manufacturing tasks. However, the company soon discovered a major problem: Many of the workers could not do simple arithmetic. A workforce that needed to operate and maintain sophisticated equipment and facilities at a zero-defect standard was often unable to calculate decimals, fractions, and percents.

A close examination of the causes revealed that many of the workers had reading problems or had learned English as a second language. They were not sufficiently proficient in English, and this detracted from their ability to read, understand, and comply with written instructions. This was one reason that they did so poorly on the general math tests that were administered to them. So how had they been able to get by up to now? One reason was that the middle management team and their own peer group were able to explain things to them verbally, often in their own language—Polish, Portuguese, Spanish. However, the organization was flattening the structure, and there would be fewer people to give this assistance. Everyone would have to carry his or her own weight. In addition, many of the workers had been with the company for a long time, and Motorola had no intention of getting rid of them. So it quickly implemented training programs to teach people how to read and solve mathematical problems, while changing its new hire program and requiring seventh-grade math and reading skills.

This new policy created problems because the company found that it often had to screen forty or fifty applicants before it found one who could meet a seventh-grade minimum requirement and also pass a drug test. With other companies in the area also recruiting from among the local labor force, Motorola knew that it would not take long before the company ran out of potential hires. So it decided to develop a strategy for getting its workforce up to educational standards. This was accomplished by teaming up with local junior colleges to provide remedial education to the employees and to develop technical training courses to complement those being offered in-house. As a result of these efforts, MU is now one of the largest and most innovative educational institutions in the world. And it likes to point out that while it has no football team, its university press prints more than one million pages a month!

A New Training Paradigm Focus Has Emerged

Today MU has created a new training and education focus. This has been accomplished through a number of steps. One is the development of a clear mission statement that serves to direct overall efforts. MU's mission is:

> to be a major catalyst for change and *continuous improvement* in support of the corporation's *business objectives*. We will provide for our clients the best value, leading edge *training and education* solutions and systems in order to be their *preferred partner* in developing a Best-in-Class workforce.

Another step has been the careful identification of developments that are necessary to unlock the training and education door. These have been learned the hard way and are likely to continue to guide the company's efforts. They include the following:

- ► Get the commitment and involvement of everyone in the organization to the training effort, beginning with those at the top.
- ► Link all training and education programs to corporate initiatives such as reducing cycle time or improving customer service.
- ► Be sure that all policies that set expectations related to training and education are carefully tracked and monitored.
- ► Create curricula that form an integrated system that can deliver consistent messages across all levels and functions.

▸ Before launching new training and education efforts, be sure that cultural and readiness issues have been carefully considered.

▸ Be sure that the workforce has the prerequisite skills before beginning new training and education programs.

A third step is to continually update and upgrade training so that it remains in sync with the demands being placed on the personnel. A good example is provided by the contrast in Table 1-2.

A fourth step is the way in which MU has set specific quality training goals that it intends to pursue into the twenty-first century. These include: (1) increased emphasis on quality in service, support, and administrative areas; (2) best-in-class software engineering; (3) senior executive programs that are focused on implementing change at a much more rapid pace; and (4) the continued development of tools for cycle time reduction.

Table 1-2. Motorola's quality training programs and development efforts: 1980s vs. 1990s.

The 1980s	The 1990s
Benchmarking	Finance metrics
Total cycle time	Motorola Management Institute (MMI)
Design for manufacturability	Focused MMI for suppliers and customers
Design for assembly	Application consulting team
Statistical process control	Managing for continuous improvement
Short-cycle manufacturing	Utilizing the six steps to six sigma
Supplier training	Senior Executive Program: Action learning
Total customer satisfaction I	College of Software Engineering and Technology
Understanding six sigma	Quality system review training
Total customer satisfaction II	Product Development Institute
Design for quality software	Six Sigma Research Institute

Source: Motorola, 1996.

Collectively, these changes have helped MU redefine the training program by busting the old paradigm and creating a new one. In the process, training has helped drive out old myths and point the way toward CVA strategies. Simply put, it's a whole new ballgame at Motorola because the company has been able to rethink its approach to getting things done and to create customer-driven programs that keep it on the cutting edge. One way it was able to start this process was by recognizing the impact of the sales manager's statement that "quality stinks," identifying areas where performance needed to be improved, and developing the necessary programs for doing so. One of the key steps in this process was an evaluation of the organizational culture, a topic that will be the focus of attention in Chapter 2.

Examining Your Own Organizational Performance

Has your organization recognized that its environment is changing and new ways of doing things are replacing the old ways? Does your company employ customer-value-added concepts in its operations? Is training a key element in your overall strategy? In answering these questions in more depth, read and respond to each of the following three assignments, and ask other members of your management team to do the same.

Assignment 1: On a scale of 1 (do not believe) to 10 (believe strongly), use your organization's current operating philosophy to rate each of the following statements:

Quality is the job
of the quality   Quality is
control department   everyone's job
  1   2   3   4   5   6   7   8   9   10

Training doesn't   Training costs
cost; it saves   a great deal
money   of money
  10   9   8   7   6   5   4   3   2   1

New quality programs have high initial costs								The best quality programs do not have high initial costs
1	2	3	4	5	6	7	8	9	10

As quality goes up, cost actually comes down								Better quality actually costs a lot of money
10	9	8	7	6	5	4	3	2	1

Measurement of data should be kept to a minimum								All relevant data should be collected
1	2	3	4	5	6	7	8	9	10

"Perfection" should be vigorously pursued								Mistakes will happen; it's human nature
10	9	8	7	6	5	4	3	2	1

Major mistakes should be prevented and minor ones minimized								All defects, large and small, should be eliminated
1	2	3	4	5	6	7	8	9	10

In improving quality, large and small gains are necessary								Quality gains come from small, continuous steps
10	9	8	7	6	5	4	3	2	1

Quality improvement takes a lot of time								Quality doesn't take time; it saves time
1	2	3	4	5	6	7	8	9	10

Thoughtful speed can improve quality								Speed creates more problems than it solves
10	9	8	7	6	5	4	3	2	1

Instructions: Total all 10 of your response scores, and compare your score to the interpretation key that follows:

Interpretation Key

> 90–100 points: Your organization is on the cutting edge of quality understanding.
>
> 70–90 points: Your organization has not fully accepted some of the truths about quality and has some mistaken beliefs that need to be examined.
>
> <70 points: Your organization needs to review its philosophy and operating data and work to dispel the myths that currently cloud its thinking regarding quality performance.

Assignment 2: Answer the following series of questions:

A. Has your company identified any ways of adding value to the goods and services it sells? If so, when was the last time, and what are some of the things you have done over the past three years? On the basis of your performance and that of your major competitors, what conclusions can you draw regarding how well these efforts are doing? In particular, are you gaining or losing market share vis-à-vis the competition? What about sales growth? What about return on investment?

_____

_____

_____

_____

_____

_____

_____

B. On the basis of your answers to question A, what conclusions can you draw? (Whatever they are, be sure to keep these responses nearby, because we will be revisiting them in Chapter 2.)

_____

_____

_____

_____

_____

_____

Assignment 3: Answer the following questions related to training:

How long has it been since your organization reviewed its training needs? What changes did you make in training at this time? Have you evaluated the effectiveness of these new efforts? What have you learned? What do you still need to find out about current programs and new programs? Have you a plan for doing all of this?

_____

_____

_____

_____

_____

_____

_____

Wrap-Up

Compare your answers to these three assignments to the responses of other members of your management team. Are your responses consistent? If not, what does this tell you? If so, now ask some of the personnel at different levels to respond to these assignments, and again compare their responses to those of you and your management team. Again, what conclusions can you reach? In particular, does your organization really believe that it's a whole new ballgame and that you are making the necessary changes to be effective in this environment?

Now put your answers to the side and begin Chapter 2. We will be returning to your responses in a little bit.

Chapter 2

Evaluate the Old Culture—and Be Prepared to Change It

An organization's culture consists of the behaviors, actions, and values that guide the way people in the enterprise behave. As the top manager in one world-class company put it, "It's the way we do business around here."

One of the major challenges many companies face when trying to remain on the competitive cutting edge is that of knowing *when* and *how* to change their cultures. Quite often the "when" part is determined by *strategy*. For example, when Motorola decided to increase its customer valued added by reducing cycle time, the company began looking into ways of redesigning work processes so that people could get things done faster. When Global Metallurgical decided to reduce its costs and become price competitive in the steel market, it started developing strategies for streamlining operations by eliminating bureaucratic work procedures and combining jobs. When Milliken realized that its Japanese competitors were able to outperform it, the company embraced the quality concept and launched its "Pursuit of Excellence Program." Simply put, strategy often serves as the initial driver in changing culture. However, if the culture is not ready for the needed change, the strategy will not be successful. Motorola conveys this idea to all personnel in its quality briefing seminars by noting that:

- ▶ When culture and strategy clash, invariably culture wins out.
- ▶ If the organizational culture does not embrace initiatives related to change, overall change efforts will fail.

In overcoming resistance to change, these organizations quickly realized that culture is like an iceberg floating in the water. Part is readily observable, but a lot of it is below the surface and not easily seen. Figure 2-1 illustrates this idea.

The initial challenge for the businesses studied in this book was to determine *how* to bring about the needed changes in a culture that was used to doing things in a way that was no longer highly competitive. In many cases this proved a major early hurdle because the pressure for change was met by strong resistance, and the companies had to develop strategies to over-

Figure 2-1. The organizational iceberg.

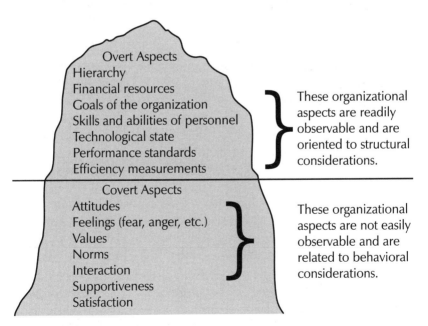

Source: Richard M. Hodgetts, *Organizational Behavior: Theory and Practice* (New York: Macmillan, 1991), p. 430.

come the pull of the status quo. In changing its own culture, Motorola used this six-step process:

1. Get top-down commitment and involvement so that senior-level management is as devoted to the new culture as are the lower-level personnel.
2. Set up a measurement system for tracking progress at both the macro and the micro levels in order to ensure that the cultural change is taking place throughout the organization.
3. Set difficult goals, and work toward them by benchmarking the best companies and then auditing the internal results on a continuous basis.
4. Give employees the education and training they need to function properly in this new culture by helping them understand *why* they are being asked to do things differently and *how* they can go about doing so.
5. Spread success stories so that those who are doing well are given credit and those who have not yet bought into the new culture begin to realize that they have to get on the bandwagon.
6. Share financial improvement gains with those who have helped bring about these gains, thus rewarding people for successful performance and encouraging them to continue their efforts.

In carrying out these steps, there are a number of different strategies that are being employed by America's most successful companies. These can be synthesized into three basic lessons:

1. *Cultural change has to begin with a careful formulation of strategic intent.* The organization has to decide what its strategy is going to be and then determine how the culture will need to be changed in order to successfully implement this plan of action.

2. *Cultural change will be sustained only if there are adequate support mechanisms.* These mechanisms take a wide variety of forms, including senior-management support, the effective communication of both what is going on and why, well-designed

training, and the judicious use of recognition and rewards. If these mechanisms are not developed and in place, the changes will be short-lived.

3. *Cultural changes have to be validated through measurement.* If the organization cannot accurately measure the changes that have occurred, it cannot state with certainty that there has been a change in culture. Conversely, if it can do these things, it can determine where and to what extent the changes have taken place and what, if anything, still needs to be done.

These three lessons incorporate what Motorola calls the "4 I's" of cultural change: (1) *inspiration*—the personnel have to be inspired to make the changes that are needed for the company to remain competitive; (2) *information*—these individuals have to be told what these changes will be, and they must be given the necessary training that will allow them to function properly in this new culture; (3) *implementation*—the changes associated with the new culture must be put into practice; and (4) *institutionalization*—the new changes must become part of the day-to-day operating processes that are used by everyone.

The following sections examine how the companies that were studied employ these three lessons to modify their organizational cultures by introducing and then institutionalizing change. When you have finished reading these three lessons, the final section of the chapter provides the opportunity to examine the extent to which these lessons are being applied in your own organization.

Lesson 1: Cultural Change Has to Begin With a Careful Formulation of Strategic Intent

Strategic intent is the *company's vision.* Basically, in a couple of words or well-chosen sentences, a statement of strategic intent sets forth an enterprise's overriding ambitions or desires that, in turn, create the basis for the organization mission and then drives its strategy. There are a variety of ways in which world-class organizations state their strategic intent. Here are four examples:

Wainwright Industries: Total customer satisfaction.

Eastman Chemical: To be the world's preferred chemical company.

Xerox: To be the leader in the global document market by providing document services that enhance business productivity.

Ames Rubber: The continuous pursuit of *Excellence Through Total Quality,* a customer- and people-centered culture that encourages participation, creativity, openness, balanced risk taking, recognition, and accomplishment of specific objectives as a way of life, will result in Ames's being acknowledged as an international benchmark in its industry segment.

Strategic Intent Focuses Cultural Change

Strategic intent provides an overriding picture of what the organization wants to accomplish. In the process, it helps identify cultural changes that have to occur. A good example is provided by Motorola. When the company decided in the late 1970s that the marketing manager's comment "quality stinks" needed to be addressed, it asked itself: What do we have to do to correct this situation? The result was a series of changes that altered the company's culture and helped drive its total quality management strategy. Table 2-1 presents some of the changes that the company introduced that ultimately changed the culture and helped make it a world-class organization capable of competing against all comers.

Xerox provides another good example of how world-class companies use strategic intent to help create a new organizational culture. As shown in Figure 2-2, the company has examined its environment in terms of four categories: the economy and society, industry and competition, technology and organization, and markets and customers. On the basis of this analysis, Xerox has identified a host of considerations that it must address if it is to remain the leader in the global marketplace by providing document services that enhance business productivity. These considerations range from an external market focus to internal organizational changes. As a result of this examination,

Table 2-1. Motorola's changing quality culture.

Decades	Changes
1970s	Acknowledgment that "quality stinks"
1980s	Naming of a corporate quality officer
	Establishment of the Motorola Training Center
	Setting of a five-year, 10x quality improvement goal
	Beginning of total defect per unit measurement in the communications sector
	Adoption of the six sigma goal
	Setting of a two-year, 10X quality improvement objective and a four-year 100X quality improvement objective
1990s	Setting of 10x defect reduction every two years
	Development of customer satisfaction metrics
	Setting of 10x improvement of cycle time in five years
	Changing of defect measurement base from parts per million to parts per billion

Source: Motorola, 1996.

Xerox has been able to set priorities, directions, and objectives. For example, the company has determined that five priorities are critical to its success: (1) customer satisfaction and loyalty; (2) motivation and satisfaction of the company personnel; (3) building of market share; (4) increasing the return on assets; and (5) increasing productivity. These are pursued in a number of ways. One is by identifying specific goals that have to be achieved. Xerox has described its goals this way:

- *Swifter.* Be more productive by doing things simpler, making quicker decisions, and bringing products to market in a shorter time period.
- *Higher.* Increase the growth rate by creating new markets, capturing larger market shares, and generating double-digit growth rates.
- *Stronger.* Develop a better customer focus by achieving a deeper understanding of customer needs, creating

Figure 2-2. Xerox: responding to the marketplace during the 1990s.

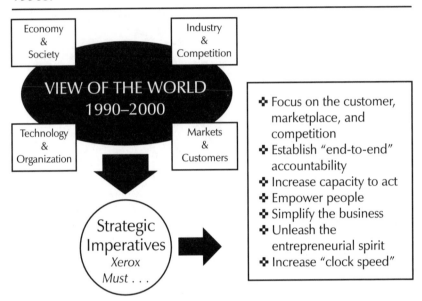

Source: Reprinted with permission of Xerox, 1997.

value, and continually doing what is right for the customer.

► *Smarter.* Find additional ways to do good work by creating enthusiastic, empowered people who are able to add value at the right time and in the right way for customers and shareholders.

All of this, of course, meant that the culture was going to have to change, but this change was likely to encounter resistance. To deal with the resistance, Xerox carefully examined the reasons change was needed, thus setting the stage for explaining and gaining support from the personnel. Xerox identified four major reasons that it had to change: (1) the marketplace for Xerox's goods and services was now global, so the company could no longer think merely in terms of U.S. or North American markets; (2) competition had become intense, and to survive in such an environment the company had to be flexible and able to respond quickly and had to have carefully segmented market niches; (3) it was important to be more efficient than ever, with an organization structure that was flatter and that used empowered and team-oriented personnel to get things done; and (4) technology was changing rapidly, so the company had to be able to offer affordable products at the point of need, and these offerings had to continue to be state-of-the-art.

Drawing together these strategic intent ideas, Xerox's change agenda calls for it to become a leader in the global document market *and* to be one of the most productive companies in the world. How can it become a global leader? The two major items on this part of the company's change agenda are: (1) become market driven and (2) maintain leadership in digital technology. How can Xerox become one of the most productive companies? The two major items on this part of the agenda are: (1) empowerment of the workforce and (2) development of productive work communities and processes. If these four change items can be achieved, the company believes it will attain new levels of productivity, market share, and sustainable, profitable growth.

Of course, the major question is *how* this can be done. While it is not easy to accomplish, strategic intent does help drive the process forward because it provides the basis for formulating objectives that are linked to the vision. In the case of an intent that also changes the culture, it gives the company a starting point for rethinking and then recasting these objectives so that they are in harmony with the new culture. At the same time, the company can look at other changes that have to occur to bring about all of this in areas such as management style, teamwork, performance, and decision making.

Lesson 2: Cultural Change Will Be Sustained Only If There Are Adequate Support Mechanisms

While cultural change begins with a careful formulation of strategic intent, much of this initial process is philosophical, conceptual and, in many cases, wishful thinking. In order to convert the intent into reality, it is necessary for world-class companies to develop support mechanisms that ensure that the change not only occurs but takes hold. A system has to be developed for *freezing* the new environmental values and behaviors. And this system has to be grounded in carefully designed support mechanisms.

Support Mechanisms Are Critical

World-class companies use a number of mechanisms to support cultural change. Six that are employed by Xerox are illustrated in Figure 2-3. These mechanisms are not unique to this company; all highly competitive companies use them in some form. They are essential because they both drive and sustain a culture change agenda. Two in particular warrant attention here because of their popularity among world-class organizations: senior management behavior and recognition and rewards. Two others, communication and standards and measures, are discussed in the next section of this chapter. The last two, transition teams and training efforts, are covered in more depth later in the book.

Change in Senior Management Behavior Is Needed

As noted earlier in the chapter, cultural change is driven from the top. This has been made particularly clear by a number of executives, including Thomas J. Malone, president and chief

Figure 2-3. Change support mechanisms at Xerox.

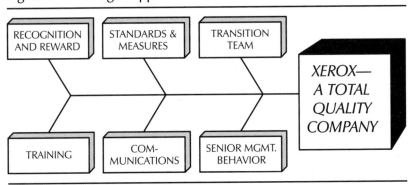

Source: Reprinted with permission of Xerox, 1996.

operating officer of Milliken, who, in an interview, noted the difficulty of getting company leadership to embrace a new approach to managing the organization and changing the culture. He put it this way:

> The only way it can change is if the number-one person—the leader—embraces those new paradigms with a passion and drive. You can't do it passively. You can't say it's a great idea and I understand it and it's worthwhile—now you guys go do it. If he does that, it doesn't work. He's not only got to embrace it, he's got to be totally involved because if he isn't, the next level of management will end up abandoning pursuit of the new paradigm.

At Xerox, senior management does get actively involved in a variety of ways, including:

- ► Acting as a role model and promoting the concept of leadership through quality
- ► Using and promoting benchmarking and employee involvement
- ► Personally using quality tools and processes
- ► Operating with a system of openness, patience, trust, and teamwork—and continually seeking feedback
- ► Fostering teamwork
- ► Inspecting operations in order to continually reinforce the need for quality output
- ► Revising promotion and selection criteria in order to promote the quality effort
- ► Using recognition and reward vehicles to reinforce change

Ames Rubber uses a similar approach. Its senior-level managers, in particular, are charged with providing leadership by setting the right tone and providing an example in both espousing the total quality management processes they have learned through training, and deploying these ideas in practice, day in and day out. In carrying out this activity, Ames has identified eight areas in which managers are expected to lead the way. These behaviors and actions are identified and explained in the fishbone diagram presented in Figure 2-4. The expected actions are similar to those prescribed for managers at Xerox, which were presented in Figure 2-3 and listed earlier.

Another way in which senior-level management at world-class companies gets involved is by actively communicating with the personnel. These companies realize that whenever a culture change has to take place, there is likely to be resistance. To deal effectively with this problem, the reasons for the change have to be explained. As Xerox likes to reminds its managers about resistance, "Major barriers are not technological, but behavioral in nature." The challenge is getting all employees to think from the customer's viewpoint and to use this awareness as a basis for acting in a different manner.

World-class companies also make wide use of communication vehicles such as open-door policies, management/associate communications meetings, and both organizationwide and departmental publications that convey what is happening and why it is happening. These publications are also important because they help promote recognition for those who are doing a good job, thus serving to highlight success and reinforce new behaviors. In fact, recognition and rewards are a critical element of all cultural change programs.

Recognition and Reward Systems Must Be Carefully Designed

While recognition and reward systems are discussed in greater depth in Chapter 7, it is useful at this point to note that a reinforcement strategy is critical to the success of cultural change because it helps freeze desired behaviors. There are a number of ways that world-class competitive companies recognize and reward their personnel. In Table 2-2 we list some of the most common. In the main, these rewards offer little direct financial incentive. They are designed primarily to encourage the personnel to support the cultural change and to let them know that management appreciates their efforts. A good example is Zytec Corporation's use of the "Zystroke form" (see Figure 2-5). This form can be filled out by anyone who has observed

Figure 2-4. A fishbone diagram of management behaviors and actions at Ames Rubber.

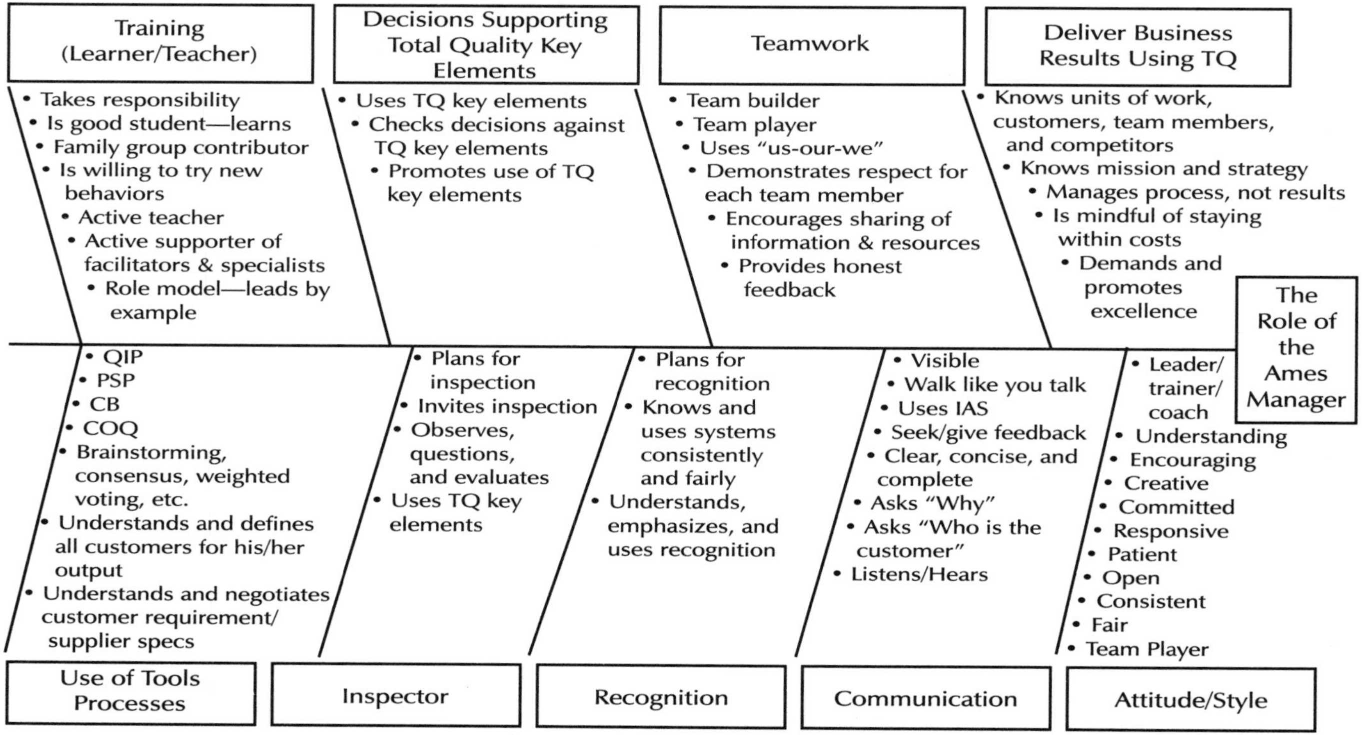

Training (Learner/Teacher)
- Takes responsibility
- Is good student—learns
- Family group contributor
- Is willing to try new behaviors
- Active teacher
- Active supporter of facilitators & specialists
- Role model—leads by example

Decisions Supporting Total Quality Key Elements
- Uses TQ key elements
- Checks decisions against TQ key elements
- Promotes use of TQ key elements

Teamwork
- Team builder
- Team player
- Uses "us-our-we"
- Demonstrates respect for each team member
- Encourages sharing of information & resources
- Provides honest feedback

Deliver Business Results Using TQ
- Knows units of work, customers, team members, and competitors
- Knows mission and strategy
- Manages process, not results
- Is mindful of staying within costs
- Demands and promotes excellence

The Role of the Ames Manager

- Leader/trainer/coach
- Understanding
- Encouraging
- Creative
- Committed
- Responsive
- Patient
- Open
- Consistent
- Fair
- Team Player

Communication
- Visible
- Walk like you talk
- Uses IAS
- Seek/give feedback
- Clear, concise, and complete
- Asks "Why"
- Asks "Who is the customer"
- Listens/Hears

Recognition
- Plans for recognition
- Knows and uses systems consistently and fairly
- Understands, emphasizes, and uses recognition

Inspector
- Plans for inspection
- Invites inspection
- Observes, questions, and evaluates
- Uses TQ key elements

Use of Tools Processes
- QIP
- PSP
- CB
- COQ
- Brainstorming, consensus, weighted voting, etc.
- Understands and defines all customers for his/her output
- Understands and negotiates customer requirement/supplier specs

| Attitude/Style | Communication | Recognition | Inspector | Use of Tools Processes |

Source: Courtesy Ames Rubber.

Table 2-2. Typical types of rewards used by world-class companies.

Plaques	Logo items (hats, shirts, pens, mugs, etc.)	Ticket to a special event
Trophies	Special parking space	Cash
Certificates	Banner for office	Pick your own gift
Letter from the CEO	Lapel pin	Special luncheon
Picture in the company newspaper	Gift certificate	Dinner with spouse or friend
Savings bond	Day off	Seminar attendance

"commendable performance" by another individual in the company. Copies are sent to the person who was responsible for the outstanding performance, the individual's immediate manager, and the president of the company. The Zystroke might result in an increase in salary or a promotion, but that is not its primary purpose. The overriding objective is to provide an opportunity for personnel to give recognition to those who are doing exceptionally good work. In many cases this psychological reward is sufficient to maintain the effort. In any event, Zytec has developed systems for evaluating the results and determining what to do in terms of follow-on to ensure that the necessary cultural changes are institutionalized. This is where validation enters the picture.

Lesson 3: Cultural Changes Have to Be Validated Through Measurement

The last step in changing culture is to answer two questions: How successful have the company's change efforts been? What else needs to be done to ensure that the company's culture more

Figure 2-5. A Zystroke form.

Zytec	**Z Y S T R O K E**
(please write firmly)	Description of commendable performance:
To:	_____
_____ NAME	_____
	_____
_____ DEPARTMENT	_____
FROM:	_____
_____ NAME	_____
	_____
_____ DEPARTMENT	_____
	_____
cc: Ron Schmidt	_____
cc: Immediate	_____
Manager	_____
	_____
	_____
	_____
	_____

White Copy, Recipient—Canary Copy, Originator—Pink Copy, President—
Goldenrod Copy, Immediate Manager

Source: Zytec Corporation. Used by permission.

fully supports the strategy needed for remaining competitive? Answers to these questions can be obtained only through the systematic measurement of results, because it is measurement that drives culture change. Motorola emphasizes and expands this idea by the following statement, taken from a recent quality briefing:

Measurement and rewards must be consistent with change objectives. What you measure is what you get.

The larger the organization, the greater the difficulty of getting the culture to change very rapidly. The president of Milliken put it this way: "The challenge in changing the culture in an organization increases exponentially with the size of the organization. Smaller organizations can move a lot faster simply because of their size and can implement these concepts rapidly." For many world-class companies, rapid change is not possible. However, necessary changes *are* accomplished because the companies know clearly what needs to be implemented and how progress can be evaluated. Basically, there are two steps in this process: (1) to the extent possible, the changes are described in quantitative terms; and (2) a system is created for gathering feedback and evaluating how well things have gone and what now needs to be done. The following sections examine these steps.

Describe the Change in Quantitative Terms

Strategic intent such as "total customer service" can be a rallying cry, but unless it is put into more specific terms, it can lose its intended effectiveness. This is why world-class companies express the changes they are hoping to accomplish in *quantifiable* and *measurable* terms. For example, when Motorola decided to become a world-class organization, it began looking into its patent application filings and realized that it was taking too long to bring an idea from conceptualization to patent application. So the company started working on a revised process designed to meet a new target. Its goal: to cut patent application time from two years to fewer than ninety days! While this was an ambitious target, it was also quantifiable and thus provided a basis for measurement.

Another example is Motorola's decision to achieve six sigma. Most companies operate at a four-sigma level, which is about 6,200 errors per million opportunities. (Some examples of average companies are provided in Figure 2-6.) By improving its performance to six sigma (3.4 errors per million), Motorola established a quantifiable target of becoming "best in class." One important aspect of achieving a six-sigma level is that as defects per million decline, so do internal and external repair costs (see Figure 2-7). Notice from the data in this figure that at four sigma, repair costs are greater than 10 percent of overall costs, but at six sigma they are less than 1 percent. This may be a difficult target to achieve, but Motorola firmly believes that "what you measure is what you get"—that the only way to change the culture and achieve ever higher levels of performance or productivity is by setting measurable targets.

Figure 2-6. Sigma levels for average companies and best-in-class.

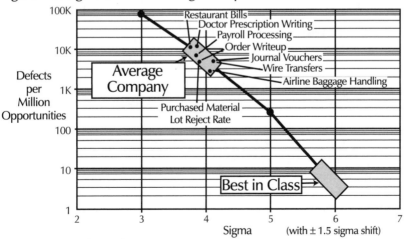

Source: Motorola quality briefing, 1996.

Figure 2-7. Internal and external repair costs for average companies and best-in-class.

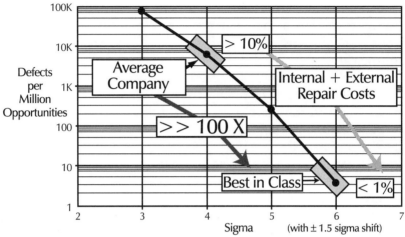

Source: Motorola quality briefing, 1996.

Evaluate the Company's Progress

The other part of the measurement process is an examination of how well things have gone and the drawing of conclusions regarding the results. Motorola and Xerox provide excellent examples of how this is done. Motorola has put together a "report card" on its performance and found that over the past nine years it has been able to:

- ► Eliminate 99.6 percent of all in-process defects
- ► Reduce the cost of poor quality by more than 84 percent on a per unit basis
- ► Achieve a cumulative manufacturing cost savings of more than $9 billion
- ► Increase employee productivity by a total of 204 percent, or 13.2 percent annually
- ► Increase product reliability by achieving an average time between failure that is five to ten times better than previously, depending on the particular product

Xerox's analysis reveals that it has: (1) cut defects per 100 machines by a factor of 10; (2) trimmed the number of production suppliers in the United States, European Union, and Pacific Rim by a factor of 10 (from 5,000 down to 400); (3) reduced defective parts on the production line by a factor of 13 (from 4,000 per million down to 300 per million); and (4) cut the inspection of incoming materials to 5 percent. At the same time, the company has been able to more than double return on assets over a six-year period. Still another measurement of the company's performance has been its productivity improvement; between 1986 and 1995 productivity increased 112 percent (see Figure 2-8). Quite clearly, the company has been able to make major changes in its culture, and bottom-line measures show that these changes are resulting in both greater profit and improved productivity.

Examining Your Own Organizational Performance

Has your organization effectively evaluated its old culture and decided how to change it? In answering this question, respond to each of the following three assignments, and ask other members of your management team to do the same.

Figure 2-8. Productivity improvement at Xerox.

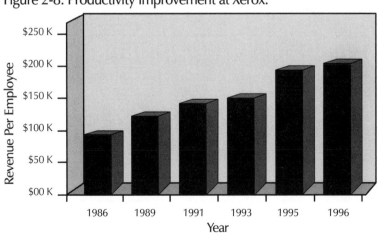

Source: Reprinted with permission of Xerox, 1997.

GOVERNORS STATE UNIVERSITY
UNIVERSITY PARK
IL 60466

Assignment 1: Answer each of the following by writing your responses directly under the question.

A. What is your company's strategic intent? Put it in your own words.

_____

_____

_____

_____

_____

B. What are the major objectives that must be attained for your organization to achieve its strategic intent? Identify at least five objectives.

_____

_____

_____

_____

_____

C. What specific cultural changes must occur in order for your organization to achieve the objectives listed above? Be as complete as possible in your answer.

_____

_____

_____

_____

_____

Assignment 2: How is your organization sustaining these new cultural changes? What forms of support mechanisms do you have in place? What new ones are you creating? In your answer, identify and describe at least the four most important support mechanisms and how each is implemented.

_____

_____

_____

_____

_____

_____

Assignment 3: How do you measure cultural change in your organization? Identify and describe at least three ways. In addition, how do you plot progress for each of these changes, and, if the results are not acceptable (or show slippage), what corrective steps are taken?

_____

_____

_____

_____

_____

_____

Wrap-Up

Compare your answers to these three assignments to the responses of other members of your management team. Are your responses consistent? If not, what does this tell you? What steps do you now need to take so that there is agreement regarding your organization's strategic intent, the cultural changes that have to take place, the supporting mechanisms that are needed to create and sustain these changes, and the measurements that can be used to track and evaluate progress?

Go back and review your responses to the assignments in Chapter 1, and compare them to those in this chapter. Is there agreement between the two sets of comments? Does your enterprise recognize the need to change and do things differently—and has it created a culture to support these changes?

Chapters 1 and 2 are designed to provide you important feedback regarding your current efforts toward becoming more competitive and the steps you are taking to ensure that the needed changes are properly implemented. These two chapters, in tandem, constitute a springboard for analyzing your organization's willingness and effort to become more quality driven. Chapter 3 focuses on the first "operating" step that world-class organizations take—an analysis of customer feedback.

Part II

Operational Steps in Measuring Quality and Achieving High Performance

In Part I we focused on how successful companies address two fundamental considerations—mind-set and culture—that are critical to both quality and high performance. These companies carry out six specific operational steps that help them target and measure quality and high performance. These steps can be viewed as part of a cyclical process that begins with targeting the customer and concludes with innovation and continuous improvement efforts that are designed to ensure that the focus remains on the customer. Of course, some of the companies described in this book place more attention on certain operational steps than do the others. For example, Motorola prides itself on the fact that everyone in the company receives a minimum of forty hours of training per year. And Wainwright Industries allocates 7 percent of its payroll for training, a percentage that is much larger than that of most world-class companies and, in Wainwright's view, helps explain why it has been able to increase its customer satisfaction levels significantly as well as drive up the number of implementable suggestions from associates. Granite Rock has created a detailed, comprehensive approach for developing associates and spends a great deal of time working with its people to ensure that they get both the equipment and the experience needed to carry out their jobs at a world-class level.

While there are a large number of specific operational steps that these companies use in achieving high performance, we have synthesized them into six separate operations, each of which is developed in a separate chapter in this section. As in the two previous chapters, you will have an opportunity to apply the operational steps and lessons to your own organization by completing the assignments at the end of each chapter.

In Chapter 3 we focus on identifying the customer, both internal and external, and finding out what this individual *really* wants. The chapter material revolves around three lessons that summarize how successful businesses do this. First, they identify the key factors that are critical to superior customer satisfaction. Second, they carefully craft forms of feedback for determining the level of this satisfaction. Third, they determine the status of the results and take necessary action for correcting errors and improving results.

The focus of Chapter 4 is on training and developing associates. Most companies continue to use the seven common tools of quality—check sheets, Pareto charts, cause-and-effect diagrams, histograms, flow charts, scatter diagrams, and control charts. Some firms are also placing increasing attention on new tools of quality such as affinity diagrams, tree diagrams, prioritization matrices, process decision program charts, interrelationship diagraphs, matrix diagrams, and activity network diagrams. In addition, there is a variety of special types of associate training programs designed to meet the specific needs of the organization. However, this is an area where much of what is happening represents fine-tuning as opposed to new paradigm thinking; a good example is the way Motorola teaches its personnel and its clients to use process mapping to sharply increase productivity.

The primary emphasis in Chapter 5 is on measuring operating results. In large degree, these efforts focus on standard feedback areas—customer satisfaction, cycle time, reject analysis, labor and equipment utilization. However, new approaches are emerging. One of the best examples is Motorola's quality system review, which now permeates the entire organization and is used, among other things, to ensure effective process operation and control.

Chapter 6 examines how these companies evaluate and develop

their employees. The primary emphasis today is changing from evaluation to development; less attention is given to identifying what associates are doing wrong and incorporating this into their performance evaluation, and more emphasis is given to finding out what people can, should, and want to do—and then helping them achieve these goals. A good example is Xerox's top-down and bottom-up evaluation, which is grounded in cultural dimensions and leadership through quality. Other good examples include General Electric's 360 degree evaluation and development process and Granite Rock's individual professional development plan process. The ways in which these are used are explained in detail in the chapter.

Chapter 7 addresses the area of rewards and recognition for accomplishments. Many businesses have problems here because they fail to reinforce associates for successful performance. The companies in this book, however, have not only developed carefully created incentives that balance financial and recognition rewards but also have built in control processes for ensuring that these programs do not lose their punch. At the end of the chapter there is a detailed questionnaire that can help you identify how well your organization is doing in this area and point out ways of correcting deficiencies.

Chapter 8 looks at how highly successful companies keep on winning. One way is through innovation—and these businesses have created some unique approaches. For example, Granite Rock's development of its "Transload Xpress" and "GraniteXpress" systems shows how customers can be serviced quickly, accurately, and profitably. And in the benchmarking area, chapter attention is focused on how companies are now developing metrics and using spiderweb diagrams to pinpoint how well they are doing and where they need to focus their improvement efforts. The last part of this chapter helps close the loop with the first chapter in the book by addressing a topic already mentioned in passing—six sigma. In revisiting this area, consideration is given to examining common logic and questioning the latter's accuracy in light of current facts.

As you read these chapters, make it a point to complete the organizational performance assignments and, on the basis of your answers and those of your personnel, develop ongoing plans for improvement. In this way, you will derive the maximum benefit from this material.

Chapter 3

Focus on the Customer: It's What You *Don't* Know That's Hurting You

Focus on the customer typically occurs throughout the operational process, but there are three times when this activity gets special attention. The first time is when the enterprise is in the throes of creating a philosophy and strategy for customer satisfaction. At this point the company typically tries to answer two key questions: How do the customers feel about our goods and services? In what key areas do we need to do well in order to maintain high satisfaction? The second time that customer focus gets careful scrutiny is when the enterprise gathers feedback from the customers. This process can take a variety of forms. Some of the most common include surveys, telephone interviews, and face-to-face conversations with buyers. The third time that customer focus gets special attention is when the results of the feedback are evaluated and decisions are made for follow-on action.

This three-step process is circular in flow. First, the key factors for customer satisfaction are determined; then they are measured; and then conclusions are drawn regarding progress and, if necessary, corrective action. However, there are a number of problems that can prevent this process from working effectively—and many world-class organizations have had to address these issues. The major problem occurs when customer feedback is insufficient and fails to identify those areas where corrective action is needed. A good example is provided by Granite Rock, which has reported that 90 percent of any company's customers never indicate that they are dissatisfied with the products or services—they simply stop doing business with the company. As a result, the company does not get the opportunity to correct its mistakes and retain the business. When IBM Rochester began developing its AS 400 minicomputer, it talked to many of its current and past customers in order to identify buyer needs. One of the questions it asked those that had stopped doing business with the company was, "What can we do to ensure that you resume doing business with us?" The responses ran the gamut from "better service" to "more reliable product." When the IBM team asked these customers what the company had done to address their concerns, they learned an interesting fact—the disgruntled customers had never said a word to the company; they had just stopped doing business with it! So, in the second step, getting feedback from customers, attention is devoted to current *and* past buyers.

The other major problem that often prevents companies from effectively using this three-step process is that too much attention is given to the technology or hardware side of the business: Does the product work properly? Does it have a good safety record? Is the failure rate within acceptable tolerances? In the process, not enough attention is given to the soft side— customer perception regarding the friendliness of the company's personnel and the ease of placing orders and getting service. When Bob Galvin heard one of his executives make the comment "quality stinks," one of things Galvin did was go out into the field and start talking to customers. In particular, he visited with individuals who were responsible for placing and receiving orders from Motorola, and he talked to them about his company's service. What he discovered was that Motorola was committing a wide variety of service errors, from improper billing to not delivering product when promised. World-class businesses focus on these types of nontechnical considerations. It's not enough to be technically correct; the customer has to feel that the company provides the support help that is needed both before and after the sale.

There are three lessons related to customer focus that come through clearly from world-class organizations. They are:

1. *Identify the key factors that are critical for superior customer satisfaction.* These key factors are typically addressed in the form of objectives that, when accomplished, will result in superior ratings in customer feedback.

2. *Carefully craft forms of feedback for determining customer satisfaction.* The most common approach is the survey instrument, but whatever form is used must provide the customer the opportunity to report both good *and* bad news and, if the company acts on this information, must result in higher customer satisfaction.

3. *Determine the status of the results, and take any necessary action for correcting errors and improving customer satisfaction.* In implementing this lesson, enterprises have to look at their performance and decide what, if anything, needs to be done now. This is accomplished by comparing the results with the objectives that were set initially.

The following sections examine how these three lessons are used by America's most competitive businesses in creating and sustaining high customer satisfaction. In particular, consideration is given to specific tools and techniques that have been specially developed by these companies.

Lesson 1: Identify the Key Factors That Are Critical for Superior Customer Satisfaction

Some companies implement this lesson by first determining what customer satisfaction means to them. For example, Motorola notes that there are two beliefs that influence the way in which it pursues total customer satisfaction: constant respect for people and uncompromising integrity. Working within these parameters, Motorola has identified three key goals that must be accomplished: (1) being best in class in regard to people, technology, manufacturing, service, marketing, product software, and hardware and systems; (2) increasing global market share; and (3) achieving superior financial results. From here, more specific and measurable targets are formulated. The following provides examples from a host of world-class companies.

Targets Should Be Specific and Measurable

AT&T Consumer Communications Services employs a variety of feedback forms to help identify service requirements. This feedback comes from satisfaction survey results, competitive analysis data, operational results, and the company's own understanding of customer requirements. These data allow AT&T to answer the question "What does the customer want, and what types of quality measures can we develop for meeting these requirements?" Through personal interaction with customers, the requirements are identified; they are then translated into quality measures by performance measurement teams. For example, in providing outstanding on-line telephone customer service, there are eight requirements that AT&T strives to meet, and in each case there are quality measures that are used to ensure that performance continues to meet or exceed customer expectations. Table 3-1 provides a description of how AT&T describes both the requirements and quality measures for phone service.

In addition, the company has identified five key customer satisfiers and in each case has committed itself to specific performance targets. Table 3-2 shows how these key customer satisfiers and company commitment are linked.

IBM uses a similar approach by first identifying those elements that are important to customer satisfaction and then linking these elements to specific areas of the organization where they can be addressed (see Figure 3-1). Next, within each of the functional areas (technical solutions, maintenance and service support, marketing/sales offerings, administration, delivery), specific performance targets are identified. For example (again, see Figure 3-1), the technical solutions personnel are responsible for quality and reliability, as well as documentation; the maintenance and service support staff are charged with, among other

Table 3-1. Customer requirements and quality measures for effective service.

Requirement	Quality Measures
Answer call quickly	Percentage of abandoned calls Measurement of average answering time (in seconds)
Helpfulness in solving problems	Percentage of customers who feel they received help in solving their problems
Complete contact accurately	Percentage of customers who feel that they accurately received a complete contact
Complete call quickly	Percentage of customers who feel that their calls were handled rapidly
Contact effectiveness	Measurement of cost/contact per minute
Courteousness	Percentage of customers who feel they were treated respectfully
Knowledgeable	Percentage of customers who feel the company personnel knew what they were doing
Offer targeted to customer needs	Measurement of needs-based selling

Source: Reprinted with permission of AT&T Consumer Communications Services, 1994.

things, seeing that there is a single contact person for handling each customer's concerns; the market/sales offerings personnel are charged with customer education; and the administration personnel are responsible for billing accuracy. Moreover, the activities of these various functional areas are coordinated between departments. This means, depending on the specific situation, that administration and the marketing and sales offices might cooperate in dealing with overlapping customer-related areas such as order accuracy, billing accuracy, and late

Table 3-2. Linking customer satisfiers and company commitment.

Key Customer Satisfiers	Company Commitment
Call quality	Unsurpassed call clarity Crisp, crystal-clear long-distance connections (TrueVoice©) Set standard for long-distance sound quality Sound quality superior to any other long-distance company
Customer service	Best service available anywhere Dedicated customer service representatives available 24 hours/day, 7 days/week Enhanced in-language services
Billing	Accurate, itemized billing Credit for misdialed calls
Reputation	Unmatched quality, service, and experience World leader in telecommunications technology Protection of the environment Technology and innovation to bring valuable new services that meet the demands of changing lifestyles
Price	Personalized savings options Affordable prices Maximized opportunities to save money off basic residential prices

Source: Reprinted with permission of AT&T Consumer Communications Services, 1994.

billings. Similarly, technical solutions and maintenance and service support problems such as product knowledge and installation and upgrades are addressed cooperatively by these two departments. And product education and product knowledge issues are dealt with by the marketing/sales offerings and maintenance and service support people working together as a team.

The key factors for customer satisfaction serve as the basis for both monitoring and taking corrective action. However, the success of this entire process depends most heavily on the data collection methods.

Figure 3-1. Customer view model.

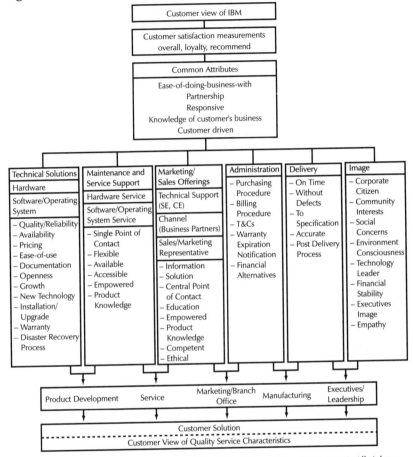

Source: © Copyright International Business Machines Corporation (IBM), 1996. All rights reserved. Reproduced with permission from IBM.

Lesson 2: Carefully Craft Forms of Feedback for Determining Customer Satisfaction

Highly competitive companies use a variety of approaches in getting feedback about customer satisfaction. The most common are surveys that ask about company performance, satisfaction with the product and/or service, and, perhaps, an overall rating of the company. Many survey instruments also give the respondent an opportunity to make personal comments in reference to questions such as, What did you like most about our product/ service? What did you like least? What would you like to see us do differently? The following sections examine some of the different types of survey instruments that are used by world-class companies.

Survey Instruments

Xerox has developed a detailed instrument designed to measure the satisfaction level of customers who make the buying decision. A copy is provided in Table 3-3.

Xerox sends out 40,000 surveys per month and has a 35 percent return rate. In particular, the company wants to find out how well it is addressing the three requirements that customers report as most critical for them: (1) Keep the equipment running; (2) fix it if it breaks; and (3) if it can't be fixed, replace it. In addition, if a customer is not satisfied with Xerox equipment, at the individual's request the company will replace it without charge with an identical model or a machine with comparable features and capabilities. This guarantee applies to all Xerox equipment acquired from the company (including purchases through sales agents, participating dealers, and retailers) and is continuously supported by Xerox or its authorized representatives under the manufacturer's warranty or a service contract.

Another way in which survey instruments are used is provided by Wainwright Industries, a small, Missouri-based manufacturer that builds precision parts and assembled systems ranging from computer disc drives to housings for electric motor applications and seat belt, sunroof, antilock brake, power antenna, and power window mechanisms. Much of the company's work requires close-tolerance machining, and its success depends heavily on customer satisfaction. In gauging this satisfaction, Wainwright relies on a specially designed customer satisfaction index (CSI) that examines both internal and external customers and measures key perceptions in communication, delivery, quality, and services. These evaluations are then used to compute an overall score. At the heart of this process is the CSI survey (see Table 3-4) that asks customers to rate the company's performance using this rating scale:

Grade	%	Conditions	Explanation
A	100	Excellent	Meets expectations; no defects of any significance
A−	90	Very good	Exceeds most expectations; minor problems, much better than average
B+	85	Above average	Meets many requirements; no significant problems; all problem causes known and solutions under way
B	80	Acceptable	Meets minimum expectations; problem causes known but solutions not developed
B−	75	Below average	Misses significant expectations; progress not clear
C	70	Not acceptable	Needs major improvements; very dissatisfied with performance
D	60	Very poor	Immediate corrective action required; critical flaws; cause of problems not recognized

On the basis of the individual scores, an overall composite rating is then computed. Here is an example of the four scores from two different surveys. Notice that Survey 1's composite results in a very poor rating, while Survey 2's rating is very good.

	Survey 1		Survey 2	
Communication	D	0	A−	90
Delivery	B+	85	A	100
Quality	B−	75	A−	90
Service	B−	75	A−	90
Overall composite	D−	58.75	A−	92.5

Customers are also asked to provide comments regarding their evaluations. If the score is low, the survey results and com-

(Text continues on page 73.)

Table 3-3. Sample customer satisfaction survey.

XEROX CUSTOMER SATISFACTION SURVEY: DECISION-MAKERS

This questionnaire should be completed by the individual who makes decisions about the acquisition of _____ . Please focus on your experiences in the product areas mentioned as you complete the questionnaire.

SECTION I: GENERAL SATISFACTION

	Very Satisfied	Somewhat Satisfied	Neither Satisfied Nor Dissatisfied	Somewhat Dissatisfied	Very Dissatisfied
1. Based on your recent experience, how satisfied are you with Xerox?	☐	☐	☐	☐	☐

	Definitely	Probably	Might or Might Not	Probably Not	Definitely Not
2. Based on your recent experience, would you acquire another product from Xerox?	☐	☐	☐	☐	☐
3. Based on your recent experience, would you recommend Xerox to a business associate?	☐	☐	☐	☐	☐

	Very Satisfied	Somewhat Satisfied	Neither Satisfied Nor Dissatisfied	Somewhat Dissatisfied	Very Dissatisfied
4. How satisfied are you overall with the quality of:					
a) Your Xerox product(s)	☐	☐	☐	☐	☐
b) Sales Support you receive	☐	☐	☐	☐	☐
c) Technical Service you receive	☐	☐	☐	☐	☐
d) Administrative Support you receive	☐	☐	☐	☐	☐
e) Handling of inquiries	☐	☐	☐	☐	☐
f) Supplies support you receive	☐	☐	☐	☐	☐
g) Xerox User Training	☐	☐	☐	☐	☐
h) Xerox Supplied Documentation	☐	☐	☐	☐	☐

Please complete 4i and 4j only if you are the decision-maker for systems products (printers, workstations, personal computers, and wordprocessors)

	Very Satisfied	Somewhat Satisfied	Neither Satisfied Nor Dissatisfied	Somewhat Dissatisfied	Very Dissatisfied
i) Your Xerox supplied software	☐	☐	☐	☐	☐
j) Xerox Systems Analyst Support	☐	☐	☐	☐	☐
k) Telephone Hotline Support	☐	☐	☐	☐	☐

SECTION II: SALES SUPPORT

	Very Satisfied	Somewhat Satisfied	Neutral	Somewhat Dissatisfied	Very Dissatisfied
5. How satisfied with Xerox Sales Representatives with regard to:					
a) Timeliness of response to your inquiries	☐	☐	☐	☐	☐
b) Frequency of contact to review your needs	☐	☐	☐	☐	☐
c) Frequency of contact to provide information about new Xerox products and services	☐	☐	☐	☐	☐
d) Product knowledge	☐	☐	☐	☐	☐
e) Application knowledge	☐	☐	☐	☐	☐
f) Understanding of your business needs	☐	☐	☐	☐	☐
g) Accuracy in explaining terms/conditions	☐	☐	☐	☐	☐
h) Ability to resolve problems	☐	☐	☐	☐	☐
i) Professionalism	☐	☐	☐	☐	☐

SECTION III: CUSTOMER SUPPORT

6. What was the purpose of your most recent call to Xerox? ☐ Inquiry ☐ Problem ☐ Haven't called, can't answer
7. How long ago did you make this call? ☐ Less than 3 months ☐ 3-6 months ☐ 6-12 months ☐ Greater than 12 months
8. What Xerox function did you contact? ☐ Sales ☐ Service ☐ Billing ☐ Collection ☐ Supplies
   ☐ Telephone Hotline Support ☐ Systems Analyst ☐ Customer Relations Group

	Very Satisfied	Somewhat Satisfied	Neither Satisfied Nor Dissatisfied	Somewhat Dissatisfied	Very Dissatisfied
9. How satisfied are you with the support you received?					
a) Ability to get to the right person(s) quickly	☐	☐	☐	☐	☐
b) Attitude of Xerox personnel who assisted you	☐	☐	☐	☐	☐
c) Ability to provide a solution	☐	☐	☐	☐	☐
d) Time required to provide a solution	☐	☐	☐	☐	☐
e) Effectiveness of the solution	☐	☐	☐	☐	☐
f) Overall satisfaction with support received	☐	☐	☐	☐	☐

10. What specific things can we do to increase your satisfaction with Xerox, our products and our services? Thank you for your feedback!

Your Name _____

Position _____

Tel # _____

Date _____

Account #
123456789

Source: Reprinted with permission of Xerox Corporation.

Table 3-4. Customer satisfaction index (CSI) survey:
Wainwright Industries

Customer: _____ Contact: _____

Rating: Rating Scale:

Communication	
Delivery	
Quality	
Service	

Grade	Conditions
A	Excellent
A–	Very good
B+	Above average
B	Acceptable
B–	Below average
C	Not acceptable
D	Very poor

Comments: _____

_____

_____

_____

_____

_____

Please return to us by _____

Thank you very much _____

Source: Reprinted with permission of Wainwright Industries.

ments are then turned over to special contact people, who are responsible for correcting these problems. In this way, proper follow-up is ensured.

Comparative Instruments

Some world-class companies employ a combination personal feedback and competitive comparison survey in which the respondents are asked to do two things: (1) Relate those factors that are most important to them when buying; and (2) identify and compare the products and/or services of organizations that they use most often. One of the best examples of comparative instrument surveys is that used by Granite Rock of Watsonville, California. The company is a construction contractor and building materials supplier; approximately once every two years, it asks its ready-mix customers to complete a survey questionnaire and to rank the importance of a number of factors that influence their purchasing of concrete. A copy of the survey questionnaire is provided in Table 3-5. The feedback allows Granite Rock to identify the order of importance of these factors and, just as critical, to compare the answers to previous years and note any changes in preferences.

In addition to using the factor form, Granite Rock sends comparative evaluation surveys to customers and noncustomers alike. The surveys are conducted by all five of the company's divisions, and mailings vary between 100 and 1,500, depending on the size of the customer base. Names are not chosen completely at random because the company wants feedback from its current buyers, especially those who have done a certain level of business with it during the previous year.

The survey asks the respondents to provide feedback on the three businesses from which they most often purchase building materials. Some of the companies that fill out this survey buy a great deal of their materials from Granite Rock, so Granite Rock can see how well it measures up against other suppliers. In other cases Granite Rock is not one of the three suppliers from whom the respondent purchases a lot of material. However, these surveys still provide important information because they give Granite Rock insights regarding how well the respondent likes its

Table 3-5. Granite Rock Company's customer survey feedback: important factors in purchasing.

What is important to <u>YOU?</u>		
Please rate each of the following on a scale from 1 to 5 with 5 being *most important* in your decision to purchase from a supplier.		
Importance	Concrete Least . . . Most	Building Materials Least . . . Most
Responsive to Special Needs	1 2 3 4 5	1 2 3 4 5
Easy to Place Orders	1 2 3 4 5	1 2 3 4 5
Consistent Product Quality	1 2 3 4 5	1 2 3 4 5
On-Time Delivery	1 2 3 4 5	1 2 3 4 5
Accurate Invoices	1 2 3 4 5	1 2 3 4 5
Lowest Prices	1 2 3 4 5	1 2 3 4 5
Attractive Credit Terms	1 2 3 4 5	1 2 3 4 5
Salespeople's Skills	1 2 3 4 5	1 2 3 4 5
Helpful Dispatchers	1 2 3 4 5	1 2 3 4 5
Courteous Drivers	1 2 3 4 5	1 2 3 4 5
Supplier Resolves Problems Fairly and Quickly	1 2 3 4 5	1 2 3 4 5
Please write in any other items not listed above which are very important to you in making your purchase decision:		

Source: Reprinted with permission of Granite Rock Company.

current suppliers and provide data that can be used in getting these businesses as customers. Referring to a noncustomer survey response, Granite Rock's marketing service manager says, "This is a really important piece of marketing intelligence. This is someone who is not in our camp whom we'd like to have in our camp. They are telling us what we need to do to get them as a customer." A copy of this comparative evaluation instrument is provided in Table 3-6.

The two instruments reproduced in Tables 3-5 and 3-6 are then combined and analyzed in arriving at an overall evaluation of the data. The way in which this is done is explained in the next section of the chapter.

Lesson 3: Determine the Status of the Results, and Take Any Necessary Action for Correcting Errors and Improving Customer Satisfaction

There are a number of ways in which world-class organizations go about evaluating results and taking the needed action. One of the most common is the use of feedback follow-up. The following section examines some examples.

Feedback Follow-Up

At AT&T Consumer Communications Services, customer-related data are analyzed and correlated with other types of information, such as operational performance results, in order to determine whether customer needs are being met or are accurate reflections of the marketplace; appropriate action is then taken. The company also carries out extensive marketing research to determine customer satisfaction and to track its own performance against that of the competition. In addition, AT&T conducts studies to gauge satisfaction for specific market segments. For example, a customer evaluation study is used to determine the relative importance of key satisfiers. The integration of this study with customer satisfaction survey ratings provides AT&T Consumer Communications Services with valuable information

Table 3-6. Granite Rock Company's supplier evaluation.

Please write in the names of the suppliers you use most often for building materials. Then grade each company using this scale:

| A = The *Best* |
| B = Above Average |
| C = *Same* as Competition |
| D = Needs Improvement |
| F = *Terrible* |

1 _____

Please write in the Building Materials Supplier you use MOST OFTEN.

2 _____

Please write in your #2 Building Materials Supplier.

3 _____

Please write in your #3 Building Materials Supplier.

1. Reliable Delivery

A. Do your orders arrive on time?			

2. Consistent Quality

A. Does the product meet your expectations?			
B. Variety of products available?			

3. Dependable Service

A. Are they responsive to special needs?			
B. Is it easy to place orders or requests with them?			
C. Are their invoices accurate?			

4. Competitive Pricing

A. Are their prices competitive?			
B. Are their credit terms competitive?			

5. People Who Care

A. Do their salespeople understand your needs?			
B. Are their dispatchers helpful?			
C. Are their drivers courteous?			
D. Do they address problems fairly and quickly?			

6. Overall Rating			

Source: Reprinted with permission of Granite Rock Company.

to support investment and resource allocation decisions designed to improve customer satisfaction. And there are a host of other steps that the organization takes. Notes a spokesperson:

> We validate internal customer satisfaction findings through independent channels, including the AT&T Consumer Advisory Panel and AT&T Consumer Advisory Panel for Disability Issues. Panel members provide feedback on policy positions or product or service offerings, and we use the feedback to improve processes. We also conduct annual Customer Advisory Council meetings to collect feedback on our potential new product and service introductions. In addition, we regularly track AT&T image, equity, and quality.
>
> Our Customer Focused Measurement Team meets monthly to evaluate our customer satisfaction determination process and key satisfiers. The team analyzes the results of customer satisfaction measures, competitive satisfaction data, customer churn, and market share. Logistical regression analysis is performed to link our customer satisfaction to market behavior.

Another example of feedback follow-up is provided by Xerox, which uses its customer survey responses as a basis for developing "countermeasures." The flow chart in Figure 3-2 illustrates how this is done. Another example is provided by the Ritz-Carlton hotel chain, which has an objective of 100 percent guest satisfaction. When something is not done in accord with the guest's wishes, an incident report is generated. After reviewing the report and other forms of customer feedback that help pinpoint guest problems or concerns, corrective action is devised.

Monitoring of Key Areas

Another way in which world-class companies evaluate results and develop follow-on strategies is through the use of key area monitoring. The Telecommunications Product Division of Corning provides an example. The division uses three methods to determine customer satisfaction: a Customer Report Card, a

Figure 3-2. Customer satisfaction: methods of measurement and results.

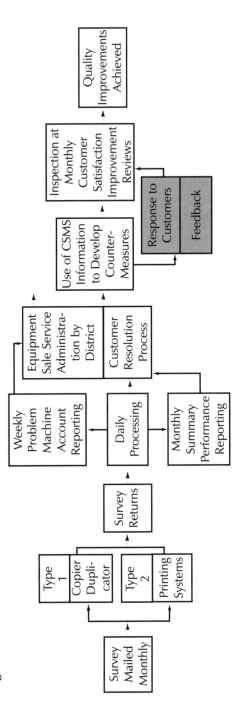

Source: Reprinted with permission of Xerox Corporation, 1996.

Customer Total Value Process, and Customer Value Assessments.

The Customer Report Card is a rating system that has been designed to help customers evaluate the Telecommunications Product Division on each of seven primary satisfaction criteria. Key domestic and international cable customers provide this feedback on a quarterly basis. These customers also rate their best supplier, so the company can identify best-supplier practices. In addition, joint venture customer satisfaction is measured on a semiannual basis through the use of a Technology Transfer Customer Survey. The objective of this survey is to gauge the level of satisfaction of key contacts at each of the company's joint ventures regarding the services and support that are provided.

Customer Total Value is a comprehensive feedback method used to obtain detailed satisfaction data in four value areas: performance, quality systems, business contribution, and supplier value. This process was developed because the company realized the need for a special measurement tool for obtaining feedback from its large strategic cable customers, who account for more than 70 percent of sales. This process is interactive in nature. Customers prepare feedback and then share it face-to-face with the company's account team. Working in tandem, the two then identify a corrective action plan to improve satisfaction in the most critical performance areas.

The Customer Value Assessment is a third-party evaluation of customer satisfaction performance. This assessment is a refinement of the Customer Report Card and the Customer Total Value processes, and it encompasses two separate sets of interviews. One is with cable customers, and the other is with end-user customers. Both are asked to evaluate the company's products, services, and customer-contact functions compared to those of the competition. Figures 3-3 and 3-4 present some of the most recent findings from these customer value assessments.

Key-area monitoring is one of the most common approaches to measuring and evaluating customer responsiveness and satisfaction. For example, Ames Rubber keeps track of repeat orders and customer dissatisfaction occurrences and charts them on a regular basis. In recent years it has found that repeat orders have

Figure 3-3. Cable customer value assessment: product and service quality.

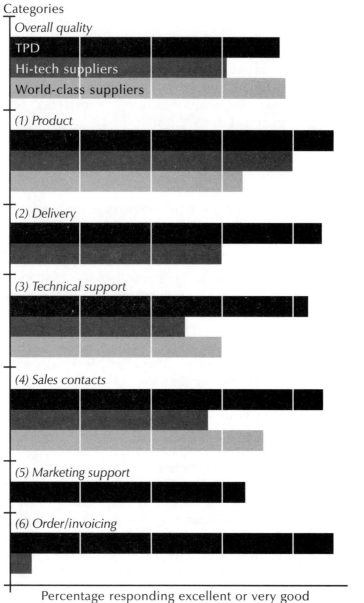

Percentage responding excellent or very good

Source: Reprinted with permission of Telecommunications Products Division, Corning Corporation.

Figure 3-4. End-user customer value assessment: product
and service quality.

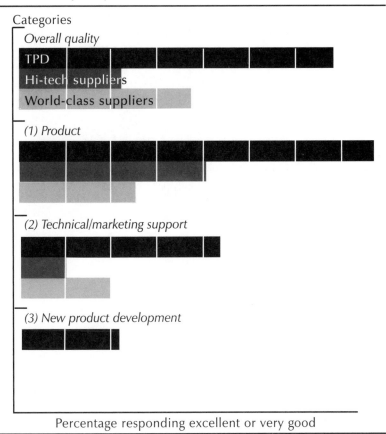

Categories

Overall quality

TPD

Hi-tech suppliers

World-class suppliers

(1) Product

(2) Technical/marketing support

(3) New product development

Percentage responding excellent or very good

Source: Reprinted with permission of Telecommunications Products Division,
Corning Corporation.

been increasing, while dissatisfaction has been dropping—clear
indications that the company's customer focus is paying off.
Meanwhile, Armstrong Building Products Operations charts the
percentage of nondefective products that it ships, as well as tracks
a customer satisfaction index for both its commercial and residential markets and for determining an overall satisfaction index.
The company also uses feedback data to create a value map that
compares the customer's quality and price perception of Armstrong products against those of competitors.

Quad Graphs

Quad graphs are two-dimensional graphs that allow companies to compare themselves to the competition on the basis of two factors. A good example is provided by Granite Rock, which combines customer ranking of purchasing factors and customer evaluation of suppliers. A skeletal diagram of the company's quad graph is provided in Figure 3-5. The vertical axis identifies

Figure 3-5. Granite rock's quad graph.

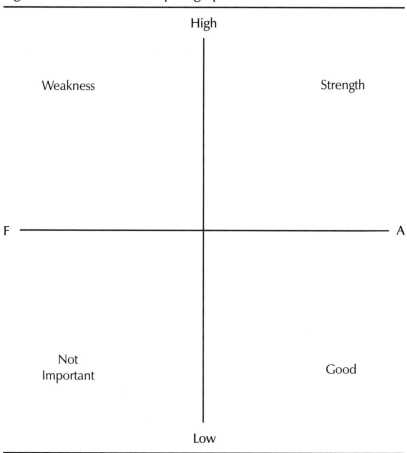

Source: Granite Rock.

those factors that are of high and low importance in the decision to purchase from a supplier. The horizontal axis identifies the grade that is given to suppliers by the customers. In each case, Granite Rock is able to compare itself to a competitor and find out how well it is doing. All data are normalized so that the average competitor ends up at the origin of the graph. As a result, considerations above the center line are more important than items below that line. Ratings to the left are below those of the average competitor, while ratings to the right are above those of the average competitor. When Granite Rock carries out its comparative evaluation using the quad graph, it wants to be to the right because this shows that it is performing better than the competitor.

The company also carries out a comparative analysis of the data in Tables 3-5 and 3-6 (pages 74 and 76) because the two are designed to reinforce each other and to help pinpoint areas of strength and weakness. For example, if a customer responds to the factor "on-time delivery" in Table 3-5 by giving it a "5" (most important) and in Table 3-6 gives one of Granite Rock's competitors a higher rating on "reliable delivery," Granite Rock can immediately see that it is not performing as well as the competitor on a factor that is very important to the buyer. On the other hand, if the buyer indicates that "lowest prices" is of least importance in purchase decisions, Granite Rock knows that it is not going to win this customer's business by trying to beat the competition on price. However, it can look down the list of factors and find out what is important to the buyer and then see how well it measures up to the competition in these areas.

In addition (again, see Table 3-5), Granite Rock uses written feedback from its customer surveys to provide further insights into how it can do a better job. Specifically, this information helps identify factors that are important in the decision-making process but are not included in the list of factors in the table.

How effective has this program been for Granite Rock? In recent years the construction business in California has declined by 43 percent, while the company's market share has grown by 88 percent. One reason is that Granite Rock has been able to identify those factors that are important to the customer and respond appropriately. For example, when Granite Rock began to measure delivery, it learned that only 68 percent of its deliveries were on time. Since then the company has improved its on-time standard to 95 percent!

Another example of the use of quad graphics is provided by Armstrong's Building Products Operations, which uses an approach similar to that of Granite Rock. Customers from each market segment are asked to rank factors according to their importance and their impact on their business. In all, Armstrong measures twelve attributes or requirements for each customer segment and then uses regression analysis techniques to determine the importance of each. On the basis of the results, the company is then able to identify high- and low-leverage issues and issues that are and are not critical. (Figure 3-6 provides an illustration.) Using the analysis, the company is able to better target its customer efforts. As a result, customer satisfaction in both the commercial and the residential markets has risen from just over 70 percent three years ago to approximately 95 percent today.

Figure 3-6. Customer segmentation at Armstrong Building Products Operations.

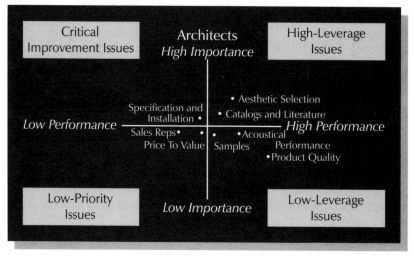

Source: Duplicated with permission of Armstrong World Industries, Inc., Building Products Operations.

Examining Your Own Organizational Performance

How effectively is your organization focusing on its customers, finding out what they *really* want, and using the information to develop strategies for improvement? In answering this question, respond to each of the following three assignments, and ask other members of your management team to do the same.

Assignment 1: Answer each of the following by writing your responses directly under the question.

A. What are the key factors that are critical for customer satisfaction in your business? How did you identify these as critical factors? How often do you evaluate and/or modify this list?

_____

_____

_____

_____

_____

_____

B. Have you identified those customer satisfaction factors that are most important? If not, why not? If so, how did you do this? How often do you review the rankings to see if the order of importance has changed?

_____

_____

_____

_____

_____

_____

Assignment 2: What type of customer feedback instrument do you use? How long has it been since you last revised the instrument? How did you link this instrument with the factors that customers told you were important to them (see Assignment 1), and what impact did the degree of importance of each factor play in your design of the instrument?

_____

_____

_____

_____

_____

_____

Assignment 3: How do you evaluate customer feedback data? What tools and techniques do you use? What types of analysis do you conduct?

_____

_____

_____

_____

_____

_____

Assignment 4: On the basis of your evaluation of customer feedback, what changes have you made in the last twelve months to improve customer satisfaction? When you measured the results of these changes, what did you find? On the basis of these results, what do you now intend to do?

_____

_____

_____

Wrap-Up

Your answers to these assignments will provide you with important feedback regarding the status of your customer focus. In particular, if you have not made any changes in your approach to improving customer satisfaction, you need to seriously question your strategy. Competitors are continually coming up with new approaches to gain and maintain customer loyalty—and so should you.

You should also be able to chart your progress and note how your organization's approach has changed. A good example is provided by IBM Rochester's quality journey. When the group first started developing the AS 400 minicomputer, the vision was focused on product reliability. Today, however, the vision is one in which customers are the final arbiters of quality, and personnel are enabled, empowered, and rewarded. Similarly, the group's early initiatives focused on the cost of quality, whereas today efforts are directed toward critical success factors and proactive customer satisfaction. And the goal of zero defects has now been replaced with an objective of undisputed leadership in customer satisfaction.

As your organization continues its efforts toward improving customer satisfaction, it should be modifying and expanding its focus. Old approaches need to be discarded or supplemented by new ones that are designed not just to create customer satisfaction but, in the words of AT&T Universal Card Services, to delight customers. One of the most important ways of ensuring that this happens is by carefully training the personnel and measuring the performance of these efforts. This subject is the focus of attention in Chapter 4.

Chapter 4

Train and Develop the Associates: Tap Their Potential and Increase Your Quality

A wide variety of training and development programs are used by the most competitive U.S. companies to increase quality and drive up performance. Some of these are designed around the seven tools of quality that are illustrated in Figure 4-1; some rely on what General Motors refers to as the "seven new tools" of quality, which are described in Figure 4-2. But most of the training is now going beyond these types of tools and focusing on teaching teamwork and problem-solving approaches that are helpful in dealing with situations and challenges unique to the specific company.

Although many of the programs focus heavily on training, there is a growing emphasis on *development* as well. The training programs are being used to teach the personnel "how to" do things; the development programs are being directed toward helping the associates improve their ability to interface effectively with customers and with each other, thus creating the basis for productive teamwork. Corning's Telecommunications Products Division provides a good example. The division has a wide range of training and development programs, including more than two hundred courses for building broad-based com-

Figure 4-1. The seven common tools of quality.

Flow Chart
Displays how a process works.

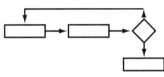

Cause & Effect Diagram
Relates causes and effects within a process.

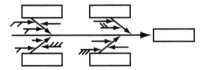

Scatter Diagram
Displays relationship between two variables.

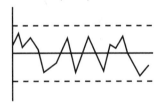

Histogram
Graphically summarizes variation within a set of data for one characteristic.

Control Chart
Identifies stability, capability and central tendency of a process.

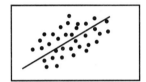

Check Sheet
Records data on a form that readily allows interpretation of results from the form itself.

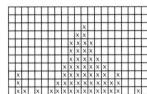

Pareto Chart
Displays frequency or cost of events to assist in determining importance.

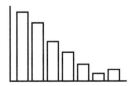

Figure 4-2. Seven new tools of quality.

Affinity Diagram
Clarifies problems by sorting language data according to their affinity.

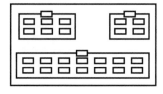

Interrelationship Digraph
Exposes related factors involved in complex, multi-variable problems.

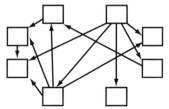

Tree Diagram
Maps out the full range of paths and tasks that need to be accomplished to achieve a primary goal and related sub-goals.

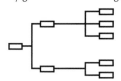

Matrix Diagram
Clarifies problems using pluralistic thinking.

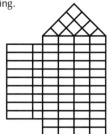

Prioritization Matrices
A combination of Tree and Matrix techniques to prioritize tasks, issues, etc. based on known weighted criteria.

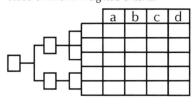

Activity Network Diagram
Used to plan the most appropriate schedule for the completion of a complex task and its related sub-tasks.

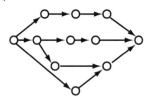

Process Decision Program Chart (PDPC)
Examines conceivable results of a proposed solution.

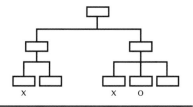

petency and approximately 150 modules for developing specific job skills. These courses and modules are designed to help individuals develop the competencies needed to carry out their jobs and also serve as the basis for an individual development plan that will help each person meet future job challenges.

For the most competitive companies, the basic development of these programs is complemented by a number of additional considerations. One is the amount of resources that the organization feels must be given over to training and development. Some businesses express this in terms of a percentage, such as 3 percent of overall sales, that will be spent on annual training and development; others use a dollar figure, such as $4.5 million annually; and still others express it in terms of time (e.g., thirty-five hours of training per employee per year).

A second consideration is the specific type of training and development that will be provided. World-class companies, in particular, opt for a combination of generic and tailor-made programs. Generic programs are typically used to teach standard concepts such as statistical process control techniques; the tailor-made ones are used to address problems or challenges unique to the organization. An example of a tailor-made program is the Ritz-Carlton's orientation program that teaches associates to remember the names of guests and to help them find where they are going in the hotel by escorting them to the location rather than just giving them verbal instructions.

A third consideration is the way in which training and development efforts are measured and evaluated. Successful businesses are continually checking on the results of their programs, identifying where things need to be modified and introducing these changes.

In carrying out the training and development programs, there are three lessons that come through clearly:

1. *Make training and development mandatory and ongoing.* Training and development are no longer options for associates. Everyone has to have it and, in a growing number of businesses, for a minimum number of hours per year. This process has two benefits for the organization. First, it forces it to continue developing in-house programs or sponsoring more outside programs.

Second, it helps ensure that the personnel will remain on the competitive cutting edge.

2. *Develop specific tools that work for the organization.* Increasingly, companies are developing training and development tools that are geared for their particular organization. Even when generic ideas are employed, they are modified to fit the specific requirements of the enterprise.

3. *Review and measure the value of the training tools.* In order to ensure that the training and development efforts are effective, bottom-line measures are identified and developed. Examples include customer satisfaction feedback, associate absenteeism and turnover, cycle time, error rates, inventory turnover, return on investment, and return on assets. These measures are used to determine how well the training is paying off and to help pinpoint areas where additional training and development can be effective.

The following sections examine some of the ways in which U.S. world-class organizations carry out these lessons. In the process, consideration is given to both the processes and the techniques that are employed.

Lesson 1: Make Training and Development Mandatory and Ongoing

Highly competitive companies implement this lesson in a variety of ways. In each case, however, they share three common characteristics: (1) Top management is strongly committed to training and is actively involved in the process; (2) training is practical and closely linked to the company's objectives and major programs so that trainees can quickly apply what they learn back on the job; and (3) a consistent training message is communicated to all levels and functions so that everyone is working in consonance.

Examples of Different Approaches

Motorola has developed a wide array of training programs for its personnel. The diagram in Figure 4-3 illustrates the com-

Figure 4-3. Strategic education at Motorola.

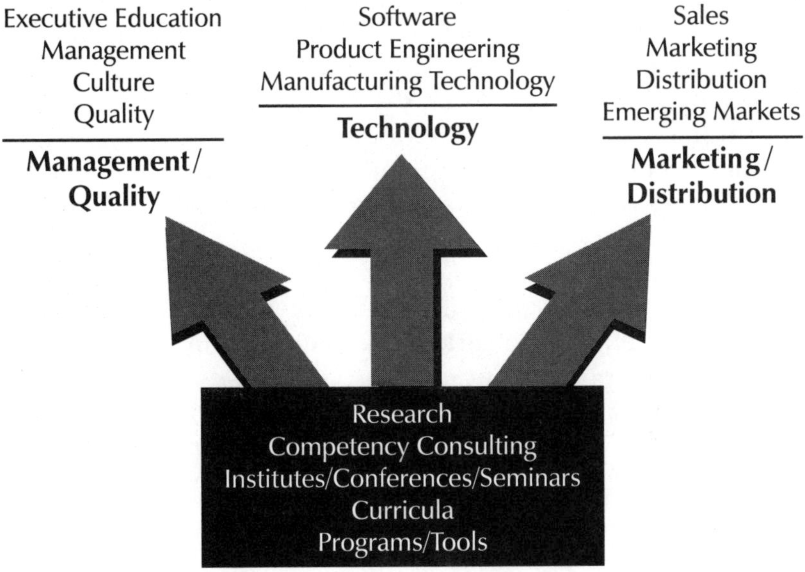

Executive Education	Software	Sales
Management	Product Engineering	Marketing
Culture	Manufacturing Technology	Distribution
Quality	**Technology**	Emerging Markets
Management/ Quality		**Marketing/ Distribution**

Research
Competency Consulting
Institutes/Conferences/Seminars
Curricula
Programs/Tools

Source: Motorola Corporation.

pany's strategic education focus. To put teeth into these programs Motorola requires attendance by *everyone*. This is clearly set forth in its corporate training and education policy:

> In order to ensure that Motorola develops and maintains a "best-in-class" workforce capable of meeting business needs, a *minimum* of 5 days of *job-relevant training* and education will be required for *every Motorola employee* each year.

In order to carry out this mandate, Motorola has training departments and groups throughout the organization. For example, there is a vice president and director of human resources for each sector and group, including Europe and Asia. In fact, there is classroom space for training at each major site around the world, including 500,000 square feet in the company's central Corporate Training Facilities. This allows the organization to offer training at all levels of the hierarchy. Figure 4-4 shows the training organization for the company at large. Working within this structure, in 1996 Motorola employed 990 full-time training professionals to provide 142,000 employees with 710,000 days of training. The cost to the company was $160 million—a sum that it feels was well invested.

One unique element of Motorola's training approach is its senior executive program (SEP), conducted annually for two hundred top managers worldwide. The company's first SEP resulted in the appointment of a corporate task force whose responsibility was to deal with the challenge of Asian competition and to rethink Motorola's off-shore manufacturing strategies. In recent years the focus of SEP has changed: It is now less a semi-

Figure 4-4. Training organization at Motorola.

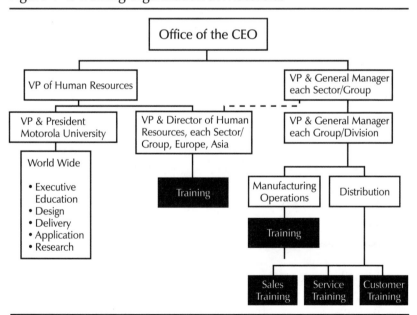

Source: Motorola Corporation.

nar and more a training program that provides participants with information they can take back to their own divisions. The topics have also become more customer focused, often covering the future needs of customers and the strategies the company can use to meet them.

At lower levels at Motorola, training programs extend from one to fifteen days and cover a wide range of topics, from the technical (manufacturing, operations, engineering) to the behavioral (time management, effective communication, leadership). These programs are held on a continual basis and are scheduled as far as twelve months in advance so that employees can work them into their schedules and thus meet the annual forty-hour education and training requirement.

At Ames Rubber all employees (or Teammates, as the company calls them) receive twenty-four hours of basic training in *Excellence Through Total Quality* at the company's dedicated training facility. Each new Teammate is assigned a "coach" who helps the individual become familiar with specific job responsibilities. The company also offers advanced technical training in a wide number of areas, including blueprint interpretations, statistical process controls, failure mode effect analysis, and spray technology. The company has a goal of forty hours of training per Teammate, at least some of which must be in advanced training. In addition, Teammates are encouraged to pursue education outside the plant through a 100 percent tuition reimbursement plan, and agreements have been established with local educational institutions to support this objective.

At Granite Rock all employees are encouraged to continue learning. The company sponsors a series of classes and speakers on a host of technical topics. In recent years employees have averaged around forty hours of training annually, which is three times more than the mining-industry average and thirteen times more than the construction-industry average. As part of Granite Rock's effort to reduce process variability and increase product reliability, employees are trained in statistical process control, root-cause analysis, and other quality-assurance and problem-solving methods. This capability allows the company to exploit the advantages afforded by investment in computer-controlled processing equipment. In fact, the company's newest batch plant features a computer-controlled process for mixing batches of concrete, thus enabling real-time monitoring of key process indicators. And with the electronically controlled system, the reliability of several key processes has now reached the six-sigma level.

At Solectron all employees receive a minimum of 160 hours of training each year. This training is broad in scope and encompasses a wide variety of tools (Pareto analysis, fishbone diagrams, control charts), computer systems, cross-functional education, and general quality training, as well as operations-focused offerings and English as a second language. The course selection, driven by the strategic planning process, is part of a broad-based curriculum created by Solectron University and strongly endorsed by senior management. (In fact, the training effort is headed by a vice president.) To identify and address training needs, an advisory committee reviews the company's strategy and business plan and then conducts a needs analysis among employees. In the process the committee reviews current worker skills and analyzes the company's technology requirements. Following this, training needs are prioritized and the needed training programs and seminars are then developed and offered. Once this is done, the organization reviews the results, and the process starts again.

At the Ritz-Carlton every new hire attends a specially designed orientation program dealing with the company's philosophy and operations. Customer service is a key focus of attention during this training. Some of the tools that are taught include teamwork and problem solving, to help associates work together to identify ways of further improving customer service, such as reducing cycle time in the restaurant and at the front desk and decreasing the time needed to bring a guest's car from the garage to the front door.

At FedEx there is a Leadership Institute that offers training for management employees, quality administrators, and facilitators. Typical Institute courses include statistical process control, skills in leading teams, and facilitator skills. Employees throughout the organization also receive quality training that is directly tied to the needs of that group.

Marlow Industries holds a series of internally developed,

management-taught training programs, two of which are professional qualification system (PQS) certification and Marlow employee empowerment teams (MEET). To obtain PQS certification, participants have to go through skills training in all job categories, followed by written and hands-on testing. All supervisors and managers must be PQS certified annually. MEET teams are responsible for identifying and solving job-related problems. Employees participate in an eleven-week training program designed to teach them the basics of team building and problem solving. Then, under the guidance of a Marlow Total Quality Council member, they meet for an hour each week to work on problems. Their solutions are presented to the TQM Council, and recognition rewards are given for significant results. Other types of training offered by Marlow include new employee orientation seminars, statistical process control training, and quality consortium courses.

Zytec offers a wide array of both mandatory and optional courses each year, some of which are taught by outside trainers. (The mandatory courses are listed in Table 4-1.) One of the most interesting is Zytec Involves People (ZIP), which teaches participants how to become team players, respond more effectively to customer needs, and reward and reinforce one another for doing a good job.

Each of these companies has made training mandatory and ongoing. And in many cases, the amount of money that is spent on training has increased annually, as have the number of mandatory hours.

Lesson 2: Develop Specific Tools That Work for the Organization

A host of training and development tools and techniques are used by U.S. world-class businesses. In some cases these offerings are fairly straightforward and easy to apply, so training requires a minimum amount of time. In other cases they are more involved and call for detailed training and practice. The following sections examine an example of each.

Table 4-1. Employee development programs at Zytec (a partial list).

All Minnesota employees hired prior to January 1, 1993, must complete this curriculum by January 1, 1996.

All Minnesota employees hired after January 1, 1993, will complete this curriculum within the first three years of employment.

The Development Center will provide refresher training and status reports for all Minnesota employees upon request.

Mandatory Courses	Class No.	Hours	Instructor				
			Manager	Development Center	Senior staff	Sales	Qualified personnel
New Hire Orientation[1]	351	08.0		✓			
Statistical Process Control	301	16.0	✓	✓			✓
QC Story	302	01.5		✓			✓
Just-in-Time Manufacturing	305	02.0	✓	✓	✓		✓
ZIP I	328	16.0		✓	✓		✓
Right to Know Refresher[2]	364	00.5	✓	✓			✓
Six Sigma	348	01.0	✓	✓			✓
Electro Static Discharge Refresher[3]	365	00.5		✓			✓
Service America	350	04.0			✓	✓	
Focus[4]	352	02.0	✓				✓
Workplace Diversity[4]	359	01.5	✓				✓
The Deming Library	360	20.0			✓		✓
Customer Action Request	358	00.5		✓			✓

[1] New hires only. Includes ESD #3, RTK #337, BBP #349, Culture #319, Safety #320, and Kanban Card (as required) #49.
[2] Annually for select personnel per Safety Department.
[3] Annually.
[4] Every three years. Focus is for non-MFEs only.

Source: Reprinted with permission of Zytec Corporation.

Investigate and Correct Operational Errors

Wainwright Industries has developed an Operation Readiness Report (ORR) that is designed to help associates both investigate and correct customer problems. A copy of the ORR is provided in Figure 4-5.

A review of the figure shows that there are eight steps that must be carried out in completing the report. Some of these steps are more challenging than others, and Wainwright associates are provided training for carrying out each of them. Here are some examples:

Step	Types of Training That Can Prove Useful
1. Form the team.	Group teamwork Communication skills
2. Describe the problem.	Affinity diagrams Cause-and-effect diagrams
3. Develop an interim solution	Prioritization matrices Interrelationship digraphs
4. Define the cause of the problem.	Matrix diagrams Scatter diagrams
5. Develop a permanent solution.	Flow charting Tree diagrams
6. Verify the solution	Pareto analysis Check sheets
7. Prevent recurrence of the problem.	Histograms Process decision program charting
8. Congratulate the team members.	Recognition of team members Allocation of rewards

When used properly, the ORR is particularly useful in identifying and resolving customer problems. It is simple to use, and if the right tools and techniques are employed at each step the results can be extremely effective. In Wainwright's case, for example, between 1992 and 1995 its customer satisfaction index

Figure 4-5. Quality team form for handling customer problems.

ORR#: _____ **Wainwright Industries Inc.** Date: _____
ORR Response Form

Description: _____

Customer No.: _____ Part No.: _____

Customer Name: _____ Originator: _____

1) Form Team:
(A small group with the process/product knowledge, allocated time, authority, and skill.)
_____

2) Describe Problem:
(Identify in quantifiable terms the who, what, where, why, how, how many for this ORR.)
_____
_____

3) Interim Corrective Action:
(Isolate the customer from the problem within 24 hours.)
_____
_____

4) Define Root Cause:
(Identify all potential causes. Verify the root cause by testing each potential cause. Identify alternative corrective actions.)
_____
_____

5) Permanent Corrective Action:
(Define and implement the best permanent corrective action. Choose ongoing controls to ensure the root cause is eliminated.)
_____
_____

6) Verification:
(Quantitatively confirm that the selected corrective actions will resolve the problem without undesirable side effects.)
_____
_____

7) Prevent Recurrence:
(Modify management systems, operating systems procedures, etc., to prevent recurrence of this and similar problems.)
_____
_____

8) Congratulate Team:
(Recognize the collective efforts of the team.)
_____
_____

Approval: _____ Date: _____

Source: Reprinted with permission of Wainwright Industries.

rose from 84 percent to more than 98 percent. There are two reasons for this. One is effective training; the other is careful integration of its ORR with customer survey feedback such as that discussed in Table 3-4, followed by vigorous evaluation and scoring of its own performance. This combination of training and feedback measurement helps explain why Wainwright's customer satisfaction index remains so high today.

Map Cross-Functional Processes

Another popular training approach is that of cross-functional process mapping. Some examples of this were provided in Chapter 1, where it was noted that "faster can sometimes be better," as seen in Motorola's reducing cycle time in the communication sector. This was accomplished by getting individuals from all of the departments that were involved in the process—from writing up the customer order, to booking it, to shipping it—to cooperate by streamlining their departmental efforts as well as cooperating with each other in handling interfunctional interfaces. The result was a cycle time reduction of almost 85 percent!

During the past few years Motorola has continued to focus on cycle time reduction—and is even using its Applications Consulting Group to market this technique to other companies around the world. In manufacturing, for example, cross-functional process mapping training is given to personnel in three areas: new product development (getting things into the market faster), producing to order (responding to demand times set by the customer), and supply management (coordinating the supply chain). By teaching personnel to flowchart the processes in each of these three areas, Motorola is able to achieve high quality, lower costs, reduced cycle time, greater flexibility, higher profits, and high customer satisfaction.

The primary objective of Motorola's training efforts is to teach participants to map the way work is being done currently and then to identify waste. (Waste includes all nonvalue-added tasks or activities *and* essential tasks and activities that are being performed at less than peak efficiency.) Working from this "as is" process map, the participants are then taught to cut the waste by:

1. Eliminating all nonvalue-added tasks and activities
2. Finding ways to perform essential tasks more efficiently, including:
   - ► Improving physical access to needed materials and information
   - ► Maintaining needed equipment so that failures are prevented
   - ► Improving lines of supervisory communication
   - ► Instituting more realistic scheduling

At first blush, this appears to be fairly obvious. However, organizations make many mistakes in designing their work flows, many of which are as much psychological as they are physical. For example, the Motorola Applications Team has found that some of its clients have departments that like to do their own testing of job applicants, even though this can be handled more efficiently through a central office such as the human resources department. However, each department feels that it can do a better job than anyone else. Result: There are people in various departments throughout the company who are duplicating tasks performed by others. An analogous example is procedures that call for managers to review reports or sign off on decisions even though these activities can be more effectively handled by others. The unwillingness to "let go" and give up some control ends up costing the company money. People find it psychologically difficult to give up power, so process mapping addresses not only what "should be" but what "must be." This includes a de-emphasis on bureaucratic rules and regulations and a willingness to empower those who are closest to the customer or who are most directly affected by a decision to play the key role in deciding how things are to be done. It also calls for those farther up the line to relinquish their hold on this authority. In the process, the time needed to get things done is often reduced substantially.

Figure 4-6 provides a conceptual view of how cross-functional process mapping works. First, the participants plot their "as is" cycle time by identifying all of the activities they carry out currently and noting the time required for each activity. Then the group works on a "should be" approach, removing nonvalue-added cycle time in the process. While this figure is only a conceptual design, it does illustrate how overall process mapping works.

Process Mapping Steps

There are number of ways of carrying out process mapping. Motorola uses eleven steps that are as complete as those used by any other company.

1. *Choose the process.* Decide the job(s) or activities that are going to be mapped so that there can be a clear-cut focus of attention.

Figure 4-6. Cross-functional process mapping: a conceptual view of "as is" vs. "should be."

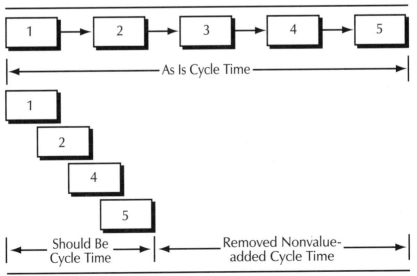

2. *Choose the champion.* Identify the person who is to "lead the charge" and be responsible for seeing that the personnel do not lose their focus or enthusiasm for the process.

3. *Choose the team.* Pick the individuals who will be responsible for studying the process and making the changes on the basis of both their expertise and their willingness to be team players.

4. *Choose an outside facilitator.* Because people who are too close to the work often have problems identifying everything they do or lack flexibility in determining how the work can be done differently, select an outsider with process mapping skills but no personal interest in the work to help facilitate the project.

5. *Empower and secure the team.* Give the group members the authority to decide what they need to do and implement these ideas without fear of being overridden by higher-level managers or concern for having their jobs or promotions threatened because of their recommendations.

6. *Conduct an "as is" session.* Map the way the job is currently being done along with the times associated with each step.

7. *Review with others.* Have nonteam members who are knowledgeable about the job review the "as is" process map and ensure that it is both accurate and complete.

8. *Conduct a "should be" session.* Map the way the job should be carried out with all nonvalue-added work eliminated and an action plan designed for making these changes.

9. *Implement the action plan.* Have the "should be" process map put into action to replace the "as is" approach being used currently.

10. *Measure the results.* Measure the outcomes from doing the job the newly designed way, and compare these to the old results.

11. *Continue to focus on continuous improvement.* Regardless of how much improvement was achieved, continue focusing on still other ways to reduce nonvalue-added work and cut cycle time still further.

Useful Guidelines

There are a number of examples that Motorola uses in its training to teach process mapping in a practical way and thus increase quality. One is to examine an activity as simple as how fast food is prepared and delivered to the customer. In this process, there are four types of activities: (1) customer-initiated behaviors such as entering the fast-food unit, placing an order, and paying for the purchase; (2) counter-related behaviors such as taking the order, collecting the cash, and giving the customer the purchase; (3) food preparation behaviors including preparing and wrapping the order; and (4) inventory-related activities such as getting the food that has been ordered and giving it to the food preparer. Participants are shown how these behaviors and activities and be diagrammed on a flow chart, along with the time required for each. Then the analysis focuses on ways to reduce the cycle time from "as is" to "should be."

During the training, participants are taught to follow a number of important guidelines in mapping jobs. One is to avoid missing any steps by having a second work group map the job, thus ensuring that the two maps are identical in terms of both work activities and associated times. A second guideline is to use an outside facilitator to help identify and challenge current procedures and bureaucratic inefficiencies. Notes one observer:

When reviewing each step, the facilitator must ask, "Why is this step being done this way?" and "Does this step add value to our product/service in the customer's mind?" If the internal operation or detail doesn't add value, the element is brought into question and, if possible, dropped.

When scrutinizing a company's business practices, the facilitator forces the company to explain the significance of each operation. Because the company under examination must provide a rationale for every step in its operation, it soon discovers (by its own admission) which steps are no longer necessary.

During the mapping process, each member of the cross-functional team is put on the hot seat by the other members, who ask the individual to prove the value-added aspect of his or her activities. As this is done, each begins to gain a better understanding of what the others do and the problems they face. This development of empathy and flow of communication is extremely useful in improving the relationships between team members, resulting in still further productivity gains. This is particularly helpful when the group is finished with its "should be" mapping and now needs to implement the new process. On the other hand, the investment is often worth the time and effort because of the substantial gains that are achieved in reducing cycle time. This becomes particularly evident during the review and measurement phase.

Lesson 3: Review and Measure the Value of the Training Tools

The value of the training should eventually be reflected in bottom-line performance. For example, thanks to statistical process controls that are applied to all product lines, Granite Rock has reduced variable costs and can produce materials that exceed customer specification and industry- and government-set standards. As a result, Granite Rock's concrete products consistently exceed the industry performance specifications by one hundred times. Other examples of measurable results are provided by Andersen Window's mass customization system and Motorola's cycle time reduction program.

Mass Customization

Andersen Windows, of Bayport, Minnesota, is a $1 billion private company whose rapid growth can be attributed largely to mass customization. This is a process of using mass production techniques to assemble items that are uniquely tailored to the demands of individual customers.

As recently as 1980 Andersen was essentially a mass producer that was turning out a wide range of standard windows in large batches. However, the market kept requesting more and more unique products. In response, the company began making modifications of its existing product line offerings. But the cost of pricing these special jobs started to rise sharply because of the time needed to make all of the calculations and drawings, as well as to price the job. Moreover, as the complexity of the products increased, so did the error rate. By 1991 Andersen was selling more than 85,000 different products, and 20 percent of all truckloads of its windows had at least one order discrepancy—a 100 percent increase from 1985.

In order to deal with this new challenge, Andersen set about creating an interactive, computerized version of its catalog and then began training its personnel as well as its retailers and distributors to use the new system. With this computerized tool, a salesperson can now help customers add, change, and take away features until they have designed a window they like. At the same time, the computer checks the window specifications for structural soundness and then generates a price quote. Thanks to training in the new system, a salesperson can now create a customer's window specs five times faster than before.

At the same time, Andersen has linked the showroom with the factory. Each retail order is transmitted directly to a company database. This allows each window to be assigned a unique number that can be tracked in real time from the assembly process to the warehouse. The computer system has also helped the company sharply reduce its error rate. As a result, in 1996 the company offered 188,000 different products, and fewer than one van load in two hundred contained an order discrepancy. The company is now turning out "batch of one" manufacturing, which is designed to dramatically reduce inventory of finished window parts. Under this arrangement, everything will be made "to order." Again, training is proving to be a critical key in Andersen's success.

Cycle Time Reduction Results

Motorola spends millions of dollars each year on employee training—and the results show that these investments pay off.

For example, here are the results Motorola was able to achieve by introducing a kanban pull system for one of its manufacturing products:

Category	Before	After	Percent Improvement
Work-in-process	5 days	.5 days	90
Defect/unit	.17	.06	65
Hours/unit	.81	.49	40
Units/sq. ft.	.6	4.4	633
Inventory space required (sq. ft.)	1,450	800	45
Shipments/week	850	3,500	312

What is particularly interesting is that not only did cycle time drop sharply, but so did the warehouse space needed for inventory storage. At the same time, inventory on the factory floor (work-in-process) was dramatically reduced, while shipments per week more than tripled. These results show that the training is being implemented effectively. However, the process and the measurement do not end here. Through continuous improvement efforts, shortcuts continue to be developed and, in some cases, the old way of doing things is abandoned and an entirely new process is created. This second step is becoming more common in recent years, as the most competitive U.S. firms conclude that process mapping can reduce cycle time only so far. At some point, no additional time savings can be extracted from the process the way it is currently being done; the only way to further reduce cycle time is by creating a new "should be" process map.

Examining Your Own Organizational Performance

How effectively is your organization training and developing its associates? In answering this question, respond to each of the following six assignments and ask other members of your management team to do the same. Then compare your answers.

Assignment 1: Answer each of the following by writing your responses directly under the set of questions.

A. How much training and development did the average person in your company receive each year? Has this increased or decreased over the last three years? If you were able to answer these two questions, how did you gather the data? If you were not able to answer this question, what steps will you take to correct this problem?

_____

_____

_____

_____

_____

_____

B. On what basis does your organization determine the amount of formal training and development that will be done each year: percentage of sales, number of hours, etc.? How does your approach compare with that of your major competitors?

_____

_____

_____

_____

_____

_____

Assignment 2: What types of training has your organization developed (or had created for it) that are tailor-made and designed to meet the specific needs of your operations? Is this type of training more common than generic training such as basic statistical process control techniques (see Figure 4-1)? Is your approach the same as that of your major competitors, or do they make greater use of tailor-made (or generic) training than you do?

_____

_____

_____

_____

_____

_____

Assignment 3: Do you have formal processes or techniques for measuring the effectiveness of your training and development programs? What percentage of these programs are evaluated on an annual basis? Is your evaluation more heavily quantitative or qualitative in nature? Also, what are some of the specific results or outcomes that you measure?

_____

_____

_____

_____

_____

_____

Assignment 4: Over the last three years, how many of your training and development programs have you modified or scrapped on the basis of an evaluation of their outcomes? What new ones have you substituted, and are the measured results of these satisfactory? What is the basis for your answer?

_____

_____

_____

_____

_____

_____

Assignment 5: On the basis of the results of your training and development efforts over the last thirty-six months, what are your plans for the future in this area? Are these efforts based on feedback you have received from your customers, or are they a result of changes that the competition has made and that you are following?

_____

_____

_____

_____

_____

_____

Assignment 6: What is the major lesson your organization has learned over the past three years regarding how to develop, implement, and evaluate training and development programs? How do you intend to use this lesson to remain competitive over the next three years? Be complete in your answer.

_____

_____

_____

_____

_____

_____

Wrap-Up

Your answers to the assignment questions will offer useful insights into how well you are applying the lessons that were examined in this chapter. In particular, there are three things that you need to keep in mind about training and development programs.

First, these programs are effective only to the extent that they help your people do a better job than the competition. If you are simply copying your competitors, you are not doing anything more than they are doing. You need to work on moving ahead, not just maintaining the status quo.

Second, training has to be tied very closely to operations. At the lower levels, the focus should be on "how to" do things. At the middle and upper levels the emphasis should be on broad areas, from the behavioral (the communication, motivation, and leading of associates) to the environmental (competitive analysis, industry trends, and strategic planning).

Third, and usually most critical, serious attempts must be made to measure the results of the training and development efforts on both a short-term and a long-term basis. If you measure only the short term (sixty days or less), the full impact of technical training is often missed because it often takes more time for people to master new tools and techniques. Conversely, in the short run the results of behavioral training are often overrated because participants are enthusiastic about applying the new ideas—but they gradually lose interest in them and go back to their old way of doing things. So long-term measurements are also important, because they indicate the true value of the programs.

The major question is: How do you measure these results? Where possible, quantitative feedback should be obtained, although this is not always easy to do, as in the case of development programs designed to improve behavioral performance. For this reason, bottom-line measures are often a useful compromise. For example, it may be difficult to measure whether a particular leadership training program has improved a manager's ability to interact well with his or her personnel by simply watching the individual in action. However, if bottom-line measures such as the unit's quality and quantity of output and levels of tardiness and absenteeism are reviewed and are improving month after month, one could conclude that the manager's leadership style is more effective now than before and that the program has had beneficial results.

In the next chapter the focus of attention is on measuring operating results. As such, it ties in very closely with the material in Lesson 3 of this chapter and helps show that training and development programs are closely linked to overall operating performance.

Chapter 5

Measure the Operating Results: Forget the Anecdotes, Look at the Facts

One of the primary ways that the most competitive U.S. companies evaluate their progress is by measuring operating results. Usually this means focusing on performance in key result areas (KRAs) or tracking key result indicators (KRIs) that impact on the bottom line. For example, Corning, Inc., has identified a host of KRIs that measure results in areas that are important to its efforts to become world-class. These measures include customer deliverables, process efficiency, and customer and employee satisfaction. The measures also help Corning focus on additional operational result areas such as return on equity, operating margin, market share, and new product development. In addition, the KRIs provide Corning with feedback on its continuous improvement efforts that can then be used for ongoing assessment and future action planning.

Obviously, the choice of which KRAs or KRIs to evaluate varies depending on the nature of the company. In all cases, however, these measures tend to be tailor-made. For example, GTE Directories is particularly interested in measuring its published error rate, since the number of mistakes in its directories is a direct indicator of quality. In recent years the company has achieved a published error rate of around 350 per 1 million list-ings—a truly outstanding result. The company also measures errors per 1,000 paid items and uses industry benchmark studies to help evaluate the result—and the latter show that the company rates best-in-class in this category. Other areas of operational performance measures for GTE include revenue growth, customer satisfaction, and preference in primary markets for its directories against those of competitors.

These criteria are fairly standard operating performance measures. However, they are not all-inclusive. World-class companies also measure nonfinancial results, such as associate feedback related to working conditions, management effectiveness, and personal concerns in the workplace. These measures are internal in focus and help the enterprise evaluate how well it is running the company from the viewpoint of the personnel.

Regardless of how these companies measure their operating results, however, two basic lessons guide their efforts:

1. *Decide what should be tracked.* These results can be qualitative and/or quantitative. It makes no difference, just as long as they are focused on key areas for performance. Typical examples include standard output measures (quality, quantity, error rates), service quality feature measures (on-time delivery, customer complaints, invoice adjustments), and quality system review measures (new product development, human resource involvement, supplier control).

2. *Systematically gather and evaluate these data.* The complementary lesson to the first is to get feedback on each of the key result areas and use it to determine how well things are going—and what now needs to be done. These data typically fall into two areas: (a) direct operating results as measured by profits, productivity, cost, and similar outcomes, and (b) feedback from customers and associates as measured by satisfaction indexes and feedback related to employee satisfaction with working conditions, management effectiveness, and work group interaction.

The following sections examine how the most competitive businesses use these two lessons to measure operating results and to create action plans for dealing with the needed changes.

The last section of the chapter provides the opportunity for you to apply these ideas to your own organization.

Lesson 1: Decide What Should Be Tracked

As noted in Chapter 1, what gets measured gets done. And the key to effective measurement is to identify those outputs or results that provide the most accurate and useful feedback on operating performance and then carefully monitor each. There are a number of ways this is done by these companies.

Choose a Focus

In some cases, tracking is focused on standard output performance. In other cases, the emphasis is on identifying key result areas and the measurement of how well things are going in each area. In still others, detailed procedures are created for the purpose of breaking down each quality area into its components and then measuring the results through a carefully designed point system. The following sections provide examples of these approaches.

Evaluate Standard Output Performance

All of the companies researched for this book gather and measure data on standard output. Wainwright Industries provides a typical example. Ten of the areas where it continually monitors performance are:

1. Customer complaints
2. Customer satisfaction
3. Piston insert market share
4. Market penetration of automotive drawn
       housing market
5. Equipment utilization
6. Labor utilization
7. Quality costs

8. Product lead time
9. Cycle time for financial statement closing
10. Reject analysis

GTE Directories also tracks ten areas: (1) listing-transaction productivity; (2) listing-error identification and resolution; (3) paper inventory; (4) directory distribution; (5) billings and collections; (6) advertisers per sales representative; (7) annual expense growth; (8) cost containment; (9) remittance-processing productivity; and (10) vendor transactions. In each case, the company gathers at least three years' data in order to gain a clear picture of overall performance. It then compares this information to internal and/or external best-in-class benchmarks. A good example is paper costs for the printing plants. Since 1992 GTE Directories has employed a roll-inventory management system that has sharply reduced paper costs. It has also installed an automated control process for distributing directories to new and transferring telephone company customers. The new system has allowed GTE to reduce delivery time from more than 120 hours to twenty-four hours.

The Ritz-Carlton tracks daily quality production reports, with information gathered from 720 work areas in its hotel systems. Examples include guest room preventive maintenance, check-ins with no queuing, time spent to achieve industry-best clean room appearance, and time to service occupied guest rooms.

At AT&T Universal Card Services the company gathers information related to customer inquiry management, including the average speed of answer (ASA) and the telephone abandon rate; application processing of customer requests for credit cards; payment processing; business processes, such as technology management; support services processes, such as financial management and customer acquisition management; and measurement of supplier processes, including relationship management, billing statement accuracy, and support services. Table 5-1 presents some of these product and service production and delivery measurement processes.

Texas Instrument's Defense Systems & Electronics Group (TI DSEG) focuses very heavily on delivering products on time

Table 5-1. Product and service production and delivery measurement processes at AT&T Universal Credit Card.

Processes Measured	Types of Measures	Frequency of Measure	Subset of Process Measures
Customer Inquiry Management			
18 process measures covering: telephone inquiry, claims, correspondence, settlement retrieval, company hand-offs, labeled envelopes, customer letters, and telephone disputes	Accuracy, timeliness, courtesy	20–100 daily depending on measure	Telephone inquiry, correspondence
call management	Abandoned, ASA	100%	Telephone inquiry
Application Processing			
24 process measures covering: application processing, correspondence, telephones, support, fraud transactions, and inbound and outbound collection calls	Accuracy, timeliness, courtesy	40–80 daily depending on measure	Application processing, telephone inquiry, correspondence
call management	Abandoned, ASA	100%	Telephone inquiry
Payment Processing			
9 process measures covering: address changes, exception payments, and payments	Accuracy, timeliness	100–450 daily depending on measure	Payment processing, address changes

Source: Reprinted by permission of AT&T Universal Credit Card Services.

and within cost parameters. Some of the areas that it tracks include design cycle time, product quality, product performance, inventory cycle time, waste reduction, environment improvements, energy efficiency, wiring board producibility, diamond-point optics turning, and supplier quality. In the case of supplier quality, for example, it has set a goal of reducing the number of suppliers and raising the performance requirements for the remainder.

Track Key Result Areas

The identification of key result areas (KRAs) for tracking is a complementary approach to the one just described. The main difference is that when KRAs are used, the organization tends to focus on fewer targets and proceeds from the belief that if everything is going well in these areas, operational performance is at least acceptable and probably as good as it is going to get. A good example is provided by FedEx's service quality indicators (SQIs). FedEx has used customer feedback to develop a dozen statistical measures of satisfaction and service quality. These are:

1. *Abandoned calls.* These are any phone calls where the caller does not speak with an agent but rather hangs up after ten seconds from the receipt of the call.
2. *Complaints reopened.* These include all customer complaints that are reopened because there has been an unsatisfactory resolution of the initial complaint.
3. *Damaged packages.* This includes all packages that contain visible or concealed damage, including weather or water damage.
4. *Invoice adjustments requested.* This is the number of packages for which customers request invoice adjustments, whether or not they are granted, because the company feels that such requests indicate that the customer perceives a problem.
5. *Lost packages.* This includes both missing packages and packages that have missing contents due to pilferage.
6. *Missed pick-ups.* These are the number of package pick-ups that did not take place.

7. *Missing proofs of delivery.* These are invoices that do not have proof-of-delivery paper work, which is something that the company promises to its customers with each bill.

8. *Overgoods.* These are packages that, for a number of possible reasons, lack identifying labels for the sender and the addressee and, as a result, are sent to the Overgoods Department.

9. *Right-day late deliveries.* This includes all packages that are delivered after the commitment time (no matter how small the time error) but on the day on which delivery was promised.

10. *Wrong-day late deliveries.* This comprises all packages that are delivered after the day on which delivery was promised.

11. *Traces.* These are "proof of performance" requests from customers that cannot be answered through data in the company's computer tracking system because an employee failed to electronically scan the package's identifying bar code into the computer at each point in the delivery process.

12. *International.* This is a composite score of service quality indicators that includes many of the other eleven indicators as well as other criteria that are international in focus such as customs clearance delays.

A relative weight is assigned to each SQI. The company thus not only tracks its performance for each of these quality indicators but uses the weighting system in arriving at an overall evaluation of how well it is serving the customer. These weights are identified in Table 5-2.

Use a Point System

One of the most comprehensive and carefully designed approaches to identifying key result areas is Motorola's Quality System Review, which employs a point system for evaluating results. In 1982 the company's Quality Council instituted a proc-

Table 5-2. FedEx's 12 service quality indicators.

Indicators	Weight
Abandoned calls	1
Complaints reopened	5
Damaged packages	10
Invoice adjustments requested	1
Lost packages	10
Missed pickups	10
Missing proofs of delivery	1
Overgoods (Lost and Found)	5
Right-day late deliveries	1
Wrong-day late deliveries	5
Traces	1
International	1

Source: FedEx.

ess of biennial quality system reviews, which were designed to assess each division or group in the firm. The objective of these reviews was to ensure that the quality system of each business was effective in achieving total customer satisfaction. This system was eventually expanded to include suppliers. Today the company conducts quality system reviews (QSRs) on a biennial basis at each major business unit, employing a cross-functional team of seven to eight high-level management experts from diverse parts of the company. The review typically takes one week and covers ten basic systems:

1. Quality system management
2. New product/technology/service development control
3. Supplier (internal or external) control
4. Process operation and control
5. Quality data programs
6. Problem solving techniques
7. Control of quality measurement equipment and systems
8. Human resources involvement

9. Customer satisfaction assessment
10. Software quality assurance

In each of these ten areas, the review team compares the business's present system to a perfect or ideal quality system as described in the QSR guidelines that have been prepared by the company and provided to the reviewers. Table 5-3 presents the review report that is used in arriving at the overall system.

Table 5-3. Motorola corporate quality system review report.

ORGANIZATION: DATE: TEAM LEADER:	SCORE (%)	SUBSYSTEMS RATINGS					WEIGHT	WEIGHTED TOTAL
		NO SYSTEM	SIGNIFICANT DEFICIENCY	IMPROVEMENT NEEDED	SATISFACTORY	OUTSTANDING		
		20	40	70	85	100		
SUBSYSTEMS		0	21	41	71	86		
1. Quality System Management							15	
2. New Product/Technology/Service Development and Control							10	
3. Supplier (Internal or External) Control							10	
4. Process Operation and Control							10	
5. Quality Data Programs							5	
6. Problem Solving Techniques							10	
7. Control of Quality Measurement Equipment and Systems							5	
8. Human Resources Involvement							5	
9. Customer Satisfaction Assessment							20	
10. Software Quality Assurance							10	

SYSTEM RATING

PREVIOUS SYSTEM RATING
(DATE:)

Source: Motorola Corporation.

Lesson 2: Systematically Gather and Evaluate These Data

In our description of how Motorola uses its QSR evaluation, we gave some consideration to the gathering and evaluating of results. Most companies do not have as detailed a tracking system as that employed in the QSR. However, there are a variety of approaches that are employed by world-class competitive businesses, and they all link back to the factors that were identified as critical to the success of their operations. In the main, these factors address bottom-line results such as costs, profits, return on investment, inventory turnover, and cycle time.

Determining Bottom-Line Results

There are two basic ways in which bottom-line results are typically reported. One is to convey performance outcomes in the key areas, noting changes and actions that now need to be developed. The other is to employ a more detailed presentation via the use of graphs that illustrate key changes over a particular time period (e.g., the past three years) and set the stage for future action planning. The following sections look at some select examples of these approaches.

Motorola Revisited

In Motorola's QSR process, individual scores for each element and subsystem range from 1 to 10. For example, in measuring Process Operation and Control (Subsystem 4 in Table 5-3), the reviewers investigate eleven areas. Table 5-4 provides a copy of this evaluation worksheet. Each element in the worksheet is first evaluated and placed into one of the five rating categories and then is given a specific score that fits within the range of the category. These results are then summarized into "strengths" and "opportunities for improvement," and a total QSR score is given to the business team before the reviewers leave the facility. If there are any scores lower than 7.1, corrective action responses are required from the operational managers.

(Text continues on page 126.)

Table 5-4. Quality system review evaluation work sheet: process operation and control subsystem.

ORGANIZATION: DATE: SUBSYSTEM: 4—Process Operation and Control		*FACTOR RATING (R)*							
		POOR	*WEAK*	*FAIR*	*MARG. QUAL.*	*QUALIFIED*	*OUTSTANDING*	*APPLICABILITY*	*SCORE*
NO.	*DESCRIPTION*	*0*	*2*	*4*	*6*	*8*	*10*	*(A)*	*(RxA)*
4.1	Are regular reviews of the product/process conducted, and are goals/plans established to continually improve at the required rate?								
4.2	Are the processes/products properly documented and controlled? Do they include appropriate environmental and customer requirements, and are they executed in conformance to the documentation?								
4.3	Are the required quality checks built into the operations within the manufacturing, field installation and service process, and are the resulting data maintained and promptly acted upon?								
4.4	Is the work area uncluttered and free of excess work-in-progress, supplies, debris, etc.? Is the environment conducive to producing quality work? Is proprietary information adequately protected?								
4.5	Are all pertinent methods of statistical quality control properly, effectively, and efficiently used?								
4.6	Are the procedures that control the reaction to process and product out-of-control situations adequate and effective?								
4.7	Are final acceptance procedures documented, controlled, and followed, and are all specified customer product audits conducted as required?								

ORGANIZATION:		FACTOR RATING (R)							
DATE: SUBSYSTEM: 4—Process Operation and Control		*POOR*	*WEAK*	*FAIR*	*MARG. QUAL.*	*QUALIFIED*	*OUTSTANDING*	*APPLICABILITY*	*SCORE*
NO.	*DESCRIPTION*	0	2	4	6	8	10	*(A)*	*(RxA)*
4.8	Is nonconforming material properly identified, segregated from regular production material, and properly dispositioned?								
4.9	Does a process change control system exist, and are customers informed of changes made to products and processes with customer approval, when required, prior to the change?								
4.10	Are the operators within the process provided with written work instructions, and are they trained to perform outstanding work?								
4.11	Are the receipt, handling, storage, packaging, and release of all material, including customer-provided items, at all stages specified and controlled to prevent damage or deterioration and to address obsolete material?								
								SCORE	
				Subsystem Rating (Score/10)				100	

Source: Motorola Corporation.

In order to ensure that all evaluation teams are following the same approach in their reviews, Motorola provides each team with a detailed series of considerations and scoring metrics for every subsystem. For example, as seen in Table 5-4, the first question that the evaluators examine is "Are regular reviews of the product/process conducted, and are goals/plans established to continually improve at the required rate?" In evaluating how well the business is doing in this area, the appraisal team is given detailed guidance for both evaluating the performance and assigning a score. Table 5-5 shows the information that is made available to the teams when reviewing and appraising the first subsystem. This information is also available to the businesses that are being evaluated, so both groups know how the evaluation will be focused and can prepare accordingly. In addition, the company provides both the evaluation team leader and the members with detailed guidelines regarding their roles and responsibilities.

The QSR process is also used to review suppliers. Typically a team of two to five individuals carries out the process over a period of two or three days; before the review is conducted, the supplier is given a copy of the QSR materials so that the company is aware of the areas that the reviewers will be examining and how the scoring process will be carried out. The purpose of this QSR is to assess the supplier's strengths, weaknesses, and opportunities for improvement. This information is reported to the supplier's top management at the conclusion of the survey. As with its own businesses, Motorola requires suppliers to provide a corrective action plan covering all subsystems and elements in which they receive a score lower than 7.1.

Other Examples of Evaluation Systems

Corning's Telecommunications Product Division focuses its efforts on a small number of key continuous improvement activities, including customer service, new markets, productivity improvements, cost, public responsibility, and reliable operations. Two areas of customer service that receive a great deal of attention are product returns and the meeting of customer-requested shipping dates. As seen in Figure 5-1, between 1986 and 1995 the

Table 5-5. Guidelines for evaluating question 1 of subsystem 4: process operation and control.

4.1 Are regular reviews of the product/process conducted and are goals/ plans established to continually improve at the required rate?

Considerations:

a. The organization holds regular reviews of performance to goals, such as: quality and cycle time, of products and processes with management.
b. Quality improvement and cycle time reduction plans are in place.
c. Process improvement results are in line with corporate and organizational improvement goals.

Scoring for Element 4.1

Poor: Improvement goals and plans are not established, and there are no reviews of product or process progress.

Weak: A few goals are established for quality and cycle time improvement. Reviews of products and processes are conducted infrequently.

Fair: Quality goals and improvement plans with measurement tracking are established in some areas. Performance to goal reviews are conducted in some major areas of the business. Management has plans to increase goal setting and performance tracking within the total organization.

Marginally Qualified: Improvement goals and measurements are established for many areas. Some improvement programs are meeting internal goals. Management reviews are held on products/processes for manufacturing and non-manufacturing areas in most major areas of the business.

Qualified: Product and process reviews by management are held in all areas of the organization. Goals and improvement plans, with appropriate measurement systems, exist for all products/ processes, including quality improvement and cycle time reduction plans. Product/process improvement results all reflect rates of improvement that are in line with established goals.

Outstanding: There is an exceptional goal setting and measurement system in place. Regularly scheduled reviews are held with focus on product/process improvement. All customer programs are tracked; most are exceeding goals and are funded where required.

Source: Motorola Corporation.

Figure 5-1. Examples of business results at Corning's telecommunications product division.

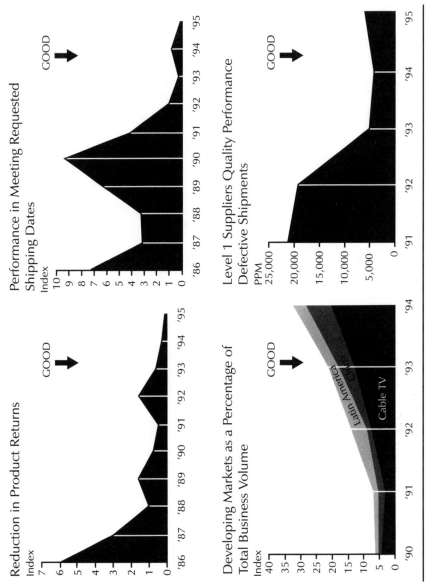

Source: Corning, Inc.

company was able to significantly improve its performance in both areas. Another area of attention has been the development of new markets as a percentage of total business volume. As also seen in Figure 5-1, the company's activity in cable television and in the Chinese and Latin American market increased sharply between 1991 and 1994 and now accounts for more than 30 percent of all business volume. Still another area of significant improvement has been the reduction in defective shipments by suppliers. From a rate of more than 20,000 parts per million (ppm) in 1991, the level has dropped sharply and is now about 20 percent of the earlier amount.

Armstrong Building Productions Operation (BPO) provides another example of how bottom-line performance is measured. The company, which is the acoustical ceiling industry's recognized leader in product and service quality, gathers data in areas such as product performance, productivity, and process effectiveness. In the case of ceiling products, for example, proper size and ease of installation are important. So the company closely monitors and controls product squareness, length, and width. As a result, dimensions and squareness claims for one family of products, which represent over half of the company's sales, have averaged only 0.25 percent of the total claims paid for all products manufactured by the company over the past five years. The building products group also develops and sells Fire Guard ceilings. These products comply with the fire-rated systems listed in the Underwriter's Laboratory Directory and, as seen in Figure 5-2, far exceed the minimum requirements for failure time. A third area that is measured is average on-time deliveries. As reported in Figure 5-2, there has been an improvement in this area of almost 700 percent (from four hours down to thirty minutes). A fourth area is productivity improvement; recent results show that output per manufacturing employee has risen by approximately 40 percent since 1992. In addition, the company measures the annual percent productivity change of hourly output for all manufacturing employees. In recent years this rate has been 200 to 300 percent greater than that reported by the U.S. Bureau of Labor Statistics for all U.S. manufacturing. BPO also measures its process effectiveness at each plant by comparing actual production to theoretical production at optimum speeds

(Text continues on page 132.)

Figure 5-2. Operating performance feedback at Armstrong's building products operations.

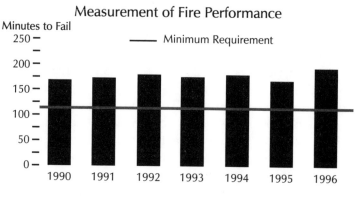

Measurement of Fire Performance

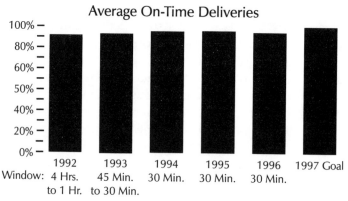

Average On-Time Deliveries

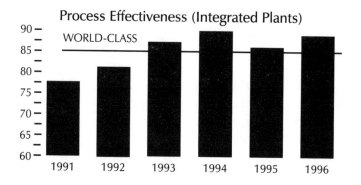

Process Effectiveness (Integrated Plants)

Source: Duplicated with permission of Armstrong World Industries, Inc., Building Products Operations.

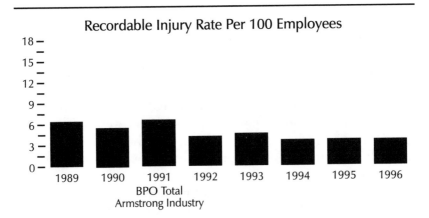

Recordable Injury Rate Per 100 Employees

BPO Total
Armstrong Industry

Change in Operating Profit
1991 as Baseline (100%)

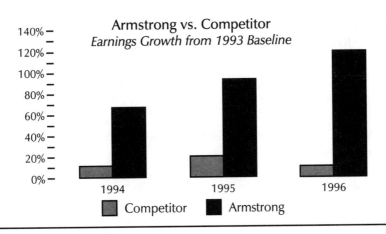

Armstrong vs. Competitor
Earnings Growth from 1993 Baseline

■ Competitor   ■ Armstrong

with zero downtime and scrap. In recent years (see Figure 5-2) the company's process effectiveness has been at world-class levels. Another measure of bottom-line results is the recordable injury rate per 100 employees. Since 1990 this rate has continued to go down and at present is approximately 20 percent of the industry average. Finally, the company measures operating profit and earnings growth as compared to those of the competition. In both cases, as seen in Figure 5-2, the trend is sharply upward; earnings growth is more than five times that of the competition.

Another good example of bottom-line results is provided by Wainwright Industries. The company constantly gathers operational performance data and uses continuous improvement to correct problems. One of the areas it focuses on is reject rates. Other indicators are more market driven and include the piston insert market share and penetration of the U.S. automotive drawn-housing market. Still others combine considerations of operational performance and customer satisfaction. Examples include customer satisfaction in both the machined products and drawn-housing markets. In each case, Wainwright plots progress on a time continuum, measuring improvements and slippages and using the information to revise its operating practices (see Figure 5-3).

Examining Your Own Organizational Performance

Has your organization clearly identified the key factors that it must track? And does it do so on a consistent and reliable basis? Even more important, what changes is the company now making in its approach to measuring operating results, and what is the logic behind these changes? In answering these questions, respond to each of the following two assignments, and ask other members of your management team to do the same.

Assignment 1: Answer each of the questions on page 135 by writing your responses directly under the questions.

Figure 5-3. Operating performance feedback at Wainwright Industries.

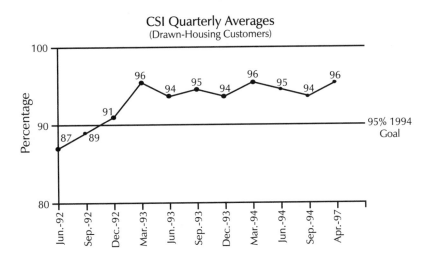

CSI Quarterly Averages
(Drawn-Housing Customers)

Quarterly Average
Customer Satisfaction Index Trend of
Drawn-Housing Customer Base

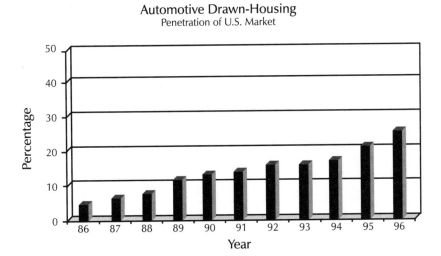

Automotive Drawn-Housing
Penetration of U.S. Market

(continues)

Figure 5-3. (continued)

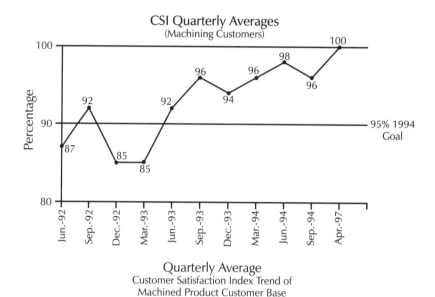

CSI Quarterly Averages
(Machining Customers)

Quarterly Average
Customer Satisfaction Index Trend of
Machined Product Customer Base

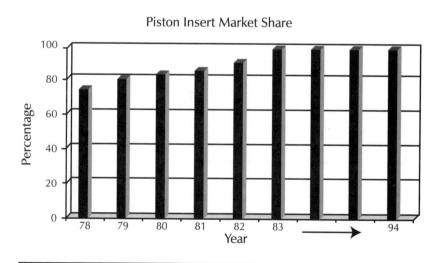

Piston Insert Market Share

Source: Reprinted with permission of Wainwright Industries.

A. Have you identified a specific set of key result factors or indicators that you use to measure operating results? What are these factors or indicators? On what basis were they chosen?

_____

_____

_____

_____

_____

_____

B. Have you identified the key result factors or indicators that are used by your competitors? Are they the same as yours? On the basis of your answers to these two questions, what conclusions can you draw?

_____

_____

_____

_____

_____

_____

C. How long has it been since you reviewed the key factors your organization uses for measuring operating results? Have these changed over the past five years? Why or why not?

_____

_____

_____

_____

_____

_____

Assignment 2: Answer each of the following by writing your responses directly under the questions.

A. How do you gather feedback data on the key operating factors you are tracking? How often is this done (daily, weekly, monthly, quarterly)? On what basis do you decide when to gather the data?

_____

_____

_____

_____

_____

B. Do you track your operating results on a time continuum? Do you compare these results with those of your competitors? If not, why not? If so, what conclusions have you been able to reach?

_____

_____

_____

_____

_____

C. On the basis of the results of your operating performance, what action plans have you formulated? How are you going to follow up and monitor these plans?

_____

_____

_____

_____

_____

Wrap-Up

The assignments in this chapter are designed to help you identify the value of your current operating measures. When you have finished answering all of the questions, you should have a clear idea of not only the key areas you are tracking but *why* you have chosen these as the ones to track. In making this evaluation, it is important to look at what the competition is tracking, because it may have found a better way. A good example, outside the scope of this book but relevant to this point, is the way in which some major companies are using economic value added to determine the true cost of their capital and, in the process, to drive up their stock market value. The way in which operating performance is tracked will change over time, and it is important to be flexible.

It is important to track data along a time continuum so that it is possible to examine changes and note trends. This is particularly true of those key factors that are not totally controlled by the organization or that involve zero-sum situations in which a gain to one company results in a loss to one or more competitors. A good example is market share.

These operating results are important measurements. However, they cannot be viewed by themselves. It is necessary also to measure personnel-related performance, which links closely to the bottom line. In Chapter 6 attention is focused on ways in which the most competitive companies are now evaluating and developing their personnel—and enhancing their bottom line in the process.

Chapter 6

Evaluate and Develop
the Personnel:
If You're Not Boundaryless,
You're Limited

One of the primary objectives of world-class companies is to get all employees working together. This means breaking down the walls between departments and creating a boundaryless company in which there is both interfunctional and intergroup cooperation. Internal customer surveys such as those used by FedEx are a good example of how companies try to break down walls between themselves and the external environment. So too are the evaluations by businesses such as the Ritz-Carlton hotel chain, which surveys its associates on an annual basis to determine both individual and overall levels of employee satisfaction. The company reports that even though it is adding thousands of new employees to its payroll every year, well over 95 percent of all associates are satisfied with the organization. And satisfied employees usually are top-performing employees.

Another example of successful feedback used to break down external and internal walls is provided by Xerox, which has been named by copious surveys as one of the top one hundred companies to work for in America. Xerox is cited for its teamwork, employee communications, and partnership with the union workforce. In addition, it ranks in the top ten in pay and benefits. These statistics clearly indicate that the company is doing an excellent job of evaluating and developing its personnel. And research shows that employee satisfaction and work performance are related. So, to the extent that an organization accurately evaluates its people and develops their talents and abilities, it also increases the likelihood that these individuals will have high work performance.

Behavior at Xerox is evaluated on the basis of an employee assessment form (which will be examined later in this chapter) that focuses on cultural dimensions such as market connectedness, action orientation, team orientation, the empowerment of people, and the use of open, honest communication. Performance is gauged in terms of business results. The results of this behavior/performance evaluation help Xerox determine those who should be replaced, those who are to be given coaching and rotation assignments, and those who will be role models and receive rewards and public recognition (see Figure 6-1).

In effectively evaluating and developing their associates,

Figure 6-1. Xerox's behavior/performance matrix.

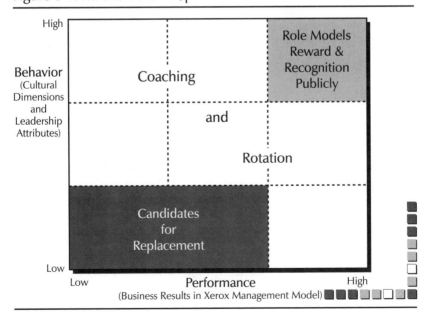

Source: Reprinted with permission of the Xerox Corporation.

companies that were the focal point of study for this book relied heavily on two lessons:

1. *Carefully and thoroughly assess personnel performance.* Assessment is done in two ways: top down and bottom up. In the classic top-down assessment, managers evaluate their associates and decide where these individuals need to improve and how they can do so. The managers also determine the types of training and experience that their people need. Tied to this are organizational policies and procedures that are employed to help ensure that assessments are fair—and that, if anyone has a question or complaint regarding how he or she has been evaluated, there is set grievance procedure. In addition, bottom-up performance evaluations are becoming increasingly common. These are designed to provide managers with feedback on how their staffs view them and to help pinpoint areas where improvement, mentoring, training, and/or development can be of value to the manager. Quite often this subordinate feedback is not limited to personal evaluations or perceptions of the manager but also focuses on critical operating areas. Examples include evaluations of the manager's business results (meets targets, tries to simplify operations), emphasis on quality (establishes improvement goals, empowers others), human resource management (inspires trust, acts fairly and equitably), teamwork (provides guidance, supports group efforts), and organizational values (acts ethically, treats everyone with dignity).

2. *Create a process for fully developing the potential of each individual.* There are a number of ways in which this lesson is implemented. The most common is for the manager to identify areas for employee improvement and to help create a strategy for ensuring that this happens. This is a fairly straightforward strategy. However, an increasing number of companies are now supplementing this approach by putting the employee in the driver's seat and letting this individual play a major role in deciding the types of development that are needed. Then, working in tandem with the manager, the person develops the strategy and the measures that will be used in evaluating his or her progress. Another, and complementary, approach is the creation of leadership development programs that help identify those

lower-level employees who have potential for management jobs and carefully train and nurture them so that they are able to move up the hierarchy.

Lesson 1: Carefully and Thoroughly Assess Personnel Performance

The companies studied for this book went about assessing personnel performance in a variety of ways. One method, used by just about all the companies, is an annual evaluation that is completed by the superior for each subordinate. A supplemental approach is to have individuals evaluate their bosses. Each manager therefore receives two sets of evaluations: one from above and one from below. A good example of this method is provided by Xerox. A second approach is the 360-degree evaluation used by companies such as General Electric.

Top-Down Evaluation at Xerox

Xerox employs a specially designed form for evaluating performance. Table 6-1 provides an illustration of the one used to assess middle-management personnel. The form is fairly brief, but there is an accompanying detailed worksheet that each rater uses in determining the assessments of cultural dimensions, leadership through quality, and leadership attributes. (Again, see Table 6-1.)

Cultural Dimensions

There are eight cultural dimensions on which each middle manager is evaluated—and the person conducting the evaluation has four choices for rating the manager on each of them: not observed, development required, competent, and role model. To guide the evaluator as well as to ensure uniformity in the evaluations of all raters, each rater is provided with a detailed description of every dimension. The eight criteria that are used in evaluating the cultural dimensions include:

Table 6-1. Management resources planning employee assessment form.

I. Employee Information			
Name	EEO/Sex	Employee No.	Hire Date
Position		Job Grade	Job Date

II. Assessment
A. Cultural Dimensions

Cultural Dimension	Not Observed	Devel. Req.	Compe- tent	Role Model		Not Observed	Devel. Req.	Compe- tent	Role Model
1. Market Connected					5. Team Oriented				
2. Absolute Results Oriented					6. Empowered People				
3. Action Oriented					7. Open and Honest Communication				
4. Line Driven					8. Organization Reflection & Learning				

B. Leadership Through Quality

	Not Observed	Devel. Req.	Compe- tent	Role Model
Leadership Through Quality				

C. Leadership Attributes

Strengths	Development Needs

III. Recommendations

A. "Stay" or Recommended Position(s)   Candidacy Status
1.   0 to 1 yr.   1-3 yrs.
2.
3.
B. Developmental Experiences/Training for
Current or Recommended Position(s)   Time Frame
1.
2.
3.

IV. Sign-off

Organization		Date Prepared
Immediate Manager	Name	Signature/Date
Second Level Manager	Name	Signature/Date
Employee's Signature*		Date

*This information is intended to assist you in your personal planning and development. It does not guarantee you will be contacted or interviewed as openings occur. Your signature indicates only that you have read the completed form, and does not necessarily mean that you agree with the contents.

Source: Reprinted with permission of the Xerox Corporation.

1. *Market connected.* Understands the technology environment within which Xerox operates; shares knowledge about competitive market conditions; delegates enough authority to meet customer requirements; keeps focused on understanding and responding to the needs of customers.

2. *Absolute results oriented.* Understands what business results are required (for example, levels of customer satisfaction, market share, time to market); defines a clear link between short-term actions and long-terms goals; strives for financial results (for example, revenue, profit, ROA, budget control); uses the vital few drivers to achieve business results; encourages continuous improvement in work processes.

3. *Action oriented.* Establishes an environment where quick response and a sense of urgency characterize all interactions; acts decisively when tough decisions are requested; ensures that decisions are implemented in a timely manner; takes calculated risks to seize business opportunities; reallocates resources quickly to respond to changing market and customer information.

4. *Line driven.* Assumes accountability for business decisions and results; resists excessive staff-driven work and limitations; translates broad strategies and objectives into line-driven activities; develops strategies that focus on the financial outcomes for the business; works to make sure that processes are line driven.

5. *Team oriented.* Recognizes the need for give and take when seeking solutions to conflict; fosters the open discussion of differences and disagreements; builds and maintains relationships across work groups; builds and maintains relationships across organizations; understands when to use teams and when to use individual contributors.

6. *Empowered people.* Avoids decisions that could be handled at a lower level; creates self-managed work teams as the way to work; motivates and supports people through effective coaching and mentoring; sets goals and monitors results, rather than getting too involved in telling people how to do things; gives credit where credit is due; delegates not only the work but the author-

ity and resources to achieve business results; is a positive role model of self-management and empowerment.

7. *Open and honest communication.* Is sensitive to the concerns and feelings of others; does not treat disagreement as disloyalty; encourages constructive feedback and dialogue; creates a climate of openness and trust through personal behavior; is willing to confront conflicts openly; actively solicits information and views from others.

8. *Organization reflection and learning.* Seeks out problems as learning opportunities; is a role model in learning and self development; actively encourages others to learn from past experiences—both successes and failures; treats new ideas with respect; encourages sharing information and knowledge; uses learnings from past experiences to redirect action.

Leadership Through Quality

In evaluating leadership through quality, the same format is employed as is used for cultural dimensions. However, in this case there is only one factor to be considered, and the focus is primarily on how well the person being evaluated applies total quality management concepts. Specifically, the evaluator is asked to assess the middle manager's commitment to leadership by determining how the individual uses quality tools to solve business problems and identify opportunities, manages by facts, conducts root causes analyses to examine all relevant data for ensuring accurate and comprehensive problem diagnoses, and serves as a role model for continuous improvement throughout the organization.

Leadership Attributes

This part of the assessment concludes with an identification of the person's strengths and development needs. In arriving at these conclusions, the evaluator is provided with a detailed work sheet that has twenty-three specific areas for consideration. These areas are grouped within four major categories as follows:

Strategic Leadership

- ► Strategic thinking
- ► Strategic implementation
- ► Customer-driven approach
- ► Inspires a shared vision
- ► Decision maker
- ► Quick study

Organizational Leadership

- ► Manages operational performance
- ► Staffs for high performance
- ► Develops organizational talent
- ► Delegates and empowers
- ► Manages teamwork
- ► Supports cross-functional teamwork
- ► Leads innovation
- ► Drives for business results
- ► Uses leadership through quality

Managing Self and Others

- ► Openness to change
- ► Interpersonal empathy and understanding
- ► Personal drive
- ► Personal strength and maturity
- ► Personal integrity

Knowledge Base

- ► Environment and industry perspective
- ► Business and financial perspective
- ► Overall technical knowledge

The evaluator follows the same pattern as was used in evaluating the cultural dimensions. A brief description of each of the twenty-three areas is provided, and the rater selects one of the four assessment choices for each area.

Recommendations for Action

On the basis of the evaluation, recommendations are made, and developmental experiences or training are suggested. What is particularly interesting about this approach to evaluation is that it is geared not merely toward identifying where the middle manager falls short but to helping create an action plan for assisting the individual to improve. This developmental focus will be discussed later in this chapter.

Bottom-Up Evaluation at Xerox

Personnel at Xerox are also given the opportunity to evaluate their managers. Each individual is provided a list of twenty-seven desired behaviors and asked to rank their superiors in terms of how often the individual exhibits each of them. These behaviors relate to leadership, teamwork, corporate values, and business results. The evaluations are computer-based, so the person making the evaluation can carry out the process quickly and easily; in addition, if the individual makes a mistake, he or she can correct it before submitting the survey.

This bottom-up evaluation is particularly helpful for developmental purposes because it helps pinpoint areas for improvement. And like other world-class organizations, Xerox is most interested in evaluation not for the purpose of identifying where errors are being made but for developing personnel talents and ensuring that mistakes are not repeated, thus tapping to the fullest the potential of each individual.

The 360-Degree Evaluation Process at General Electric

General Electric's approach to evaluation, like that of Xerox, focuses on getting feedback from more than one source. And like Xerox, the evaluation is designed to create a basis for the future development of the personnel, serving to tap each person's full potential. In the past, this was not always done. A few years ago, GE Plastics Americas surveyed its employees and received the following feedback to career-related statements:

Statement	Favorable Responses	Neutral Responses	Unfavorable Responses
My manager/supervisor provides sufficient coaching and guidance to help me achieve my work objectives.	29%	24%	47%
The most capable employees are selected for advancement and promotion.	13	21	66
My organization retains the people it will need to compete successfully in the future.	21	28	51

Obviously, the personnel did not feel that the company was doing a very good job of evaluating and developing its human resources. So GE Plastics Americas—whose vision, culture, and leadership values clearly enunciated personnel development as a priority focus—began focusing increased attention on both its evaluation and development processes. And this is where the 360-degree assessment process has proved extremely beneficial.

How the 360-Degree Process Works

General Electric's 360-degree evaluation process is an assessment that solicits multiple perspectives from a host of different sources, including each employee's direct manager, coworkers, subordinates, and, in some cases, customers, vendors, and other external sources. The objective of the process is to measure key leadership characteristics and job performance at a specific time. As a result, the 360-degree evaluation is a tool for both assessment and development planning.

In accomplishing these objectives, the first step is the establishment of a baseline against which future performance can be measured and a development action plan can be written. Then, at the end of an agreed-on time, the individual is assessed by comparing his or her performance against GE values. This seven-step process is described in Figure 6-2.

Figure 6-2. Steps in the 360-degree process.

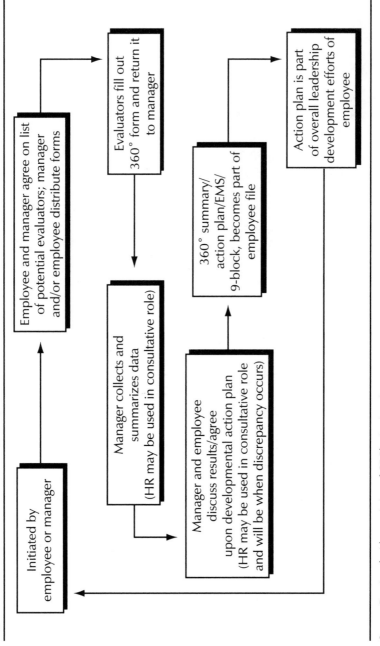

Source: Reprinted with permission of GE Plastics Americas.

The Nine-Block Matrix

Performance is based on the goals that were agreed upon for the measurement period. In this evaluation method, the focus is on *what* the person accomplished—and the result is expressed in a 1, 2, 3 numeric rating:

> 1 = Excellent performance
> 2 = Fully satisfactory performance
> 3 = Significant improvement needed

At the same time, the individual is evaluated on the *means* that were used in accomplishing these goals. This evaluation is based on how others view the person's company business values, which in the case of GE Plastics Americas includes vision, accountability, excellence, empowerment/involvement, teamwork, receptivity to change, and energy/speed. This overall evaluation is summarized in an A-B-C alphabet rating:

> A = Significant strength
> B = Some development needs
> C = Significant development required

The two ratings are then brought together in a nine-block matrix. Figure 6-3 shows the matrix used by GE Plastics Americas. This matrix is then used to summarize the person's strengths and identify developmental needs.

Lesson 2: Create a Process for Fully Developing the Potential of Each Individual

This section shows how Xerox handles the process of evaluating employees. It also looks at the approaches employed by General Electric and Granite Rock.

Developmental Action at Xerox

As shown in Table 6-1, part of the employee assessment at Xerox involves the identification of developmental experiences or

Figure 6-3. GE Plastic's nine-block matrix.

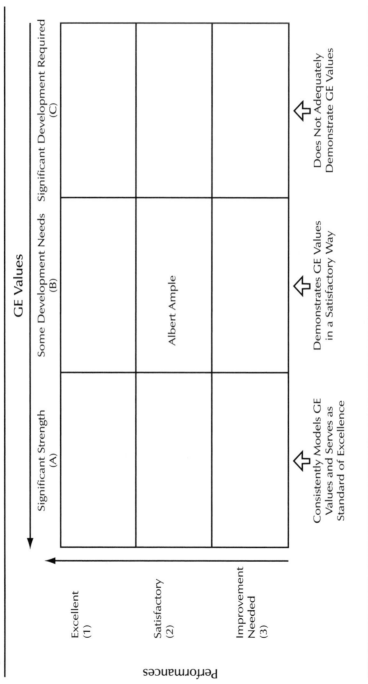

Source: Reprinted with permission of GE Plastics Americas.

training that will help the employee in his or her current or recommended position. This plan of action entails three steps: (1) determining the experiences, knowledge, and/or skills that the person requires; (2) spelling out the activities that need to be taken in meeting these needs; and (3) developing a timetable for when the actions will be taken. The form that is used in this process in illustrated in Table 6-2 and serves as the guide for implementation of the overall developmental action plan.

GE's Personnel Development Approach

The final step in the 360-degree evaluation review is the creation of a developmental action plan. This consists of a dialogue between the manager and the employee regarding long- and short-term developmental needs and the options that are available for meeting these needs. This overall developmental process is linked very closely to the company's business strategy, so all new skills, knowledge, and training will help the individual do a better job of meeting individual and team goals; in turn, these goals will assist the operating unit in attaining its goals. The development planning process begins with a careful assessment of the individual's performance, career interests, and personal skills and of the changing requirements of the person's job as shaped by the changing demands being made on the business. These issues are addressed during a developmental session between the individual and the manager in which key questions such as the following are answered:

- ► What types of performance improvement are needed? In what areas is there the greatest need for improvement?
- ► Are there any skill, knowledge, or competency gaps that need to be filled?
- ► What needs are now being created by changing job requirements or conditions? What additional needs will be created over the next five years as additional changes occur?
- ► What career directions does the employee want to pursue over the next few years?
- ► What personal motivators are not being met in the employee's current job?

Table 6-2. Developmental action plan.

DEVELOPMENTAL ACTION PLAN

NAME: ORGANIZATION/DIVISION:

JOB TITLE: GRADE:

The Developmental Action Plan (DAP) is designed to identify development activities which will contribute most to helping employees to be more effective in their present jobs and/or future positions. It is recommended that the *Skill and Personal Characteristics* definitions be used for completing this form. The creation and implementation of the DAP should be a joint effort involving the employee and his/her manager.

DEVELOPMENTAL NEEDS What experiences, knowledge, or skills are needed?	DEVELOPMENTAL ACTIONS What actions are to be taken, and by whom?	TIMETABLE When will the actions be taken?

Employee's Signature: _____   Date: _____

Manager's Signature: _____   Date: _____

Source: Reprinted with permission of the Xerox Corporation.

➤ What thinking, business knowledge, and skills will the individual need to develop in order to meet the challenges of the future?

On the basis of the developmental meeting, an action plan is developed. This plan is a result of agreement between the employee and the manager regarding the performance areas (outputs, competencies) that need improvement or that hold high payoff potential for the employee's long-term career goals. They also discuss the ways in which the employee can get the assistance that is needed. Examples include coaching, one-on-one instruction, assignment changes, task force work, project leadership, classes, courses, workshops, and personal reading assignments of books and articles.

Once the action plan has been formulated, it is the employee's responsibility to take charge and begin implementing the agreed-on steps. The manager, of course, remains available to assist, but it is the employee who is ultimately responsible for his or her own development. Then, at the end of the agreed-on time, the 360-degree evaluation process begins again. The manager uses input from a variety of sources to evaluate the individual, and this serves as the basis for the next developmental meeting.

Granite Rock's Individual Professional Development Plan Process

Despite the fact that it is a fairly small company, Granite Rock has created a very detailed, carefully crafted individual professional development plan (IPDP) that could be the envy of much larger companies. At the heart of the IPDP process is a four-page form that focuses on major job responsibilities, strengths, developmental objectives, the creation of a developmental plan, and quarterly reviews of progress.

Steps in the Process

Granite Rock's IPDP process begins with the individual employee and his or her manager or supervisor *both* completing a preliminary draft of the form for the employee. The purpose of this dual exercise is to create a basis for discussion. The two individuals then meet and discuss what each has written. The objective of this meeting is to create a revised IPDP that both parties agree will be used to guide the development of the employee. During the meeting, the manager or supervisor gets to learn more about the employee's interests in expanding his or her knowledge and/or opportunities within the company. At the same time, the manager gets the chance to make suggestions that can help the employee further develop his or her skills and abilities.

After the two have completed their revised IPDP, the consensus plan is presented at a Roundtable by the manager. Members of the Roundtable consist of other participating managers and members of the Executive Committee. The IPDP is then discussed in an open and constructive manner. Comments on the proposed developmental objectives and experiences are noted, and modifications to the plan may be made.

After the Roundtable discussion, the manager has a follow-up meeting with the employee. At this time the individual either confirms that the plan has been accepted or suggests modifications that should be made as a result of that meeting. After this is done, both individuals sign the final copy of the IPDP.

During the next twelve months the employee and the manager meet quarterly to review progress and to make any needed modifications in the developmental plan. As a result, the plan becomes the basis for constant employee improvement.

Another interesting part of the process is that copies of the IPDP are *not* placed in the individual's personnel file. There are only two copies. One is kept by the employee; the other is held by the manager.

A Sample IPDP

Figure 6-4 presents a sample plan that has been filled out by a mixer driver who is participating in the IPDP for the first time. A close look at the plan shows that she and her manager have agreed that she had four major job responsibilities and three special accomplishments during the previous year. She also has a handful of strengths (page two of the form), and there are five major developmental objectives she will be pursuing over the next year. In order to accomplish these goals (page three of the form), there are a series of things she will have to do, such as attend the Frontline Leadership module on "Dealing with Emotional Behavior," enroll in a Dale Carnegie course on public speaking and human relations, and attend a safety training program. In each case there are observable measures that will be used in determining progress. For example, she will be expected to complete the Frontline Leadership model by October 1; to illustrate that she can apply what she learned in the Dale Carnegie course, by December 1 she will have to provide the Branch Manager with two examples of how she was able to deal effectively with two dissatisfied customers.

The last page of the development plan details quarterly achievements and modifications, if any, to the plan. As indicated in the second-quarter achievements section (page four of the plan), she attended the Frontline Leadership module on June 14, which was well ahead of the October 1 deadline. And in the third-quarter achievements section she reported two instances in which she dealt effectively with two customers who had been unhappy. She completed this on September 23, well ahead of the December 1 deadline.

The sample IPDP provides an excellent illustration of how the process is used to develop personnel. At the end of the year, the process will begin again. And Granite Rock has developed a guide for helping managers lead their people through the later years of the IPDP process by showing them where to focus their attention and how to direct the meeting.

Benefits of the IPDP Process

Granite Rock's employee developmental approach benefits not only the individual but also the personnel at large and the company. The major benefits are for the individual, who is given a strong hand in determining the type of training and development goals he or she will be pursuing. As a result, the person gets a chance to promote his or her own personal growth and

(Text continues on page 160.)

GOVERNORS STATE UNIVERSITY
UNIVERSITY PARK
IL 60466

Figure 6-4. Granite Rock's IPDP.

Check as appropriate:
☐ *Individual's first draft.*
☐ *Supervisor's first draft.*
☐ *Consensus form*
   (to be brought to Roundtable).
☐ *Final Form.*

Graniterock

Individual Professional Development Plan

Name: ___Ima Driver___   IPDP Plan Year: _1 / 94_ to _1 / 95_

Position: ___Mixer Driver___   Branch/Location: _Monterey—341_

Hire Date: ___June 1, 1993___   Time in Current Position: _6 months_

A: Major Job Responsibilities: *Include major responsibilities; new responsibilities made possible by last year's development (star these with *).*

1. Operate all vehicles in a safe, courteous manner.

2. Ensure customer satisfaction by delivering the specified product to the right place at the right time.

3. Maintain daily vehicle inspection reports, assuring that each vehicle is safe and well-maintained.

4. Support the nine Corporate Objectives and all company policies while striving for continuous improvement; follow established procedures.

B: Summary of 19_93_ IPDP Results: *Include items from Section E, Column 2 of last year's IPDP, using same numbering. Precede each item with A, AM, AP, NAM or NA. Also, list other special accomplishments (star these with *).*

First year participation; no prior IPDP.

Special accomplishments:
* completed first six months of Graniterock service without any accidents or violations.
* attended driver training/vehicle inspection class.
* actively participated on Branch Driver Safety Quality Team.

10/93   GRANITE ROCK COMPANY

C: Strengths on the Job: *Include clearly exceptional strengths that are displayed consistently and new strengths added this year (star these new strengths with *).*

1. Good understanding of company objectives, policies and procedures.

2. Safety conscious; sets a strong positive example for others.

3. Strong driving skills; familiar with each make of mixer trucks in use at the Branch.

4. Sees what needs to be done and does it.

5. Seeks opportunities to learn.

D: Major Developmental Objectives: *Develop what you want to learn to do in the next twelve months. Include new skill development that can enhance job performance quality, job satisfaction, and general professional growth. Also, you may want to include new skill development that could lead to interesting new challenges. Use format: "Learn_____ so that I can_____."*

1. Learn the company's numbering system for mix designs so that I can provide even better customer service and catch potential mistakes.

2. Increase my skills in dealing with emotional people so that I can handle any unhappy customer more effectively.

3. Learn streets and terrain of the territory that I drive so that I can find the quickest, safest routes for my deliveries.

4. Learn about mix designs (what they are designed to do) so that I can answer customer questions and guard against wrong applications.

5. Learn additional safety techniques so that I can be sure to operate without personal injury or property damage.

(continues)

Figure 6-4. (continued)

E: Developmental Plan for the Period Beginning 1 / 94 *and Ending* 1 / 95 .

Column 1–Planned Experiences/Activities:

Include <u>how</u> skills will be learned, with at least one learning activity/experience per objective in Section D. Number items so as to correspond to Section D.

Column 2–Observable Measures:

Include criteria which will demonstrate that the planned activities/experiences from Column 1 have been completed <u>and</u> that each objective in Section D has been met. Include target dates.

1. Be instructed by the Branch Salesperson, Dispatcher and Manager with regard to the code patterns of mix design numbers.

1. a. Meet 1/2 hour with each person by 4/1/94.
   b. Branch Salesperson to quiz me to establish that I know all commonly used mix designs; quiz to be given by 5/1/94.
   c. By 12/1/94, report to Branch Manager at least 3 instances using my new mix design knowledge.

2. a. Attend Frontline Leadership module on "Dealing with Emotional Behavior."
   b. Enroll in Dale Carnegie course on "Public Speaking and Human Relations."

2. a. Complete Frontage Leadership module by 10/1/94.
   b. Complete Carnegie course by 8/1/94.
   c. By 12/1/94, report to Branch Manager two instances of dealing effectively with two customers who had been unhappy.

3. Study maps and drive alternate routes.

3. a. Log total of 10 hours studying maps by 4/1/94.
   b. Log comparisons of time needed to drive main route and at least one alternate route to three general areas to which we frequently deliver concrete. Do this by 5/15/94.
   c. Demonstrate to Dispatcher by 6/1/94 the ability to identify the quickest, safest route to 3 job sites. Do this by 7/1/94.

4. Enroll in PCA Concrete school in Chicago.

4. a. Complete school and pass final exam by 9/1/94.
   b. Report to Branch Manager three instances of answering customer questions regarding mix designs. Do so by 11/1/94.

5. Attend Safety training given by instructor.

5. a. Complete training by 6/1/94.
   b. Complete 1994 with zero lost-time accidents, zero preventable collisions, and zero moving violations.

(Sign below on final form after Roundtable discussion:)

_____

Manager/Supervisor   Date

_____

Individual   Date

F: Quarterly Review of Progress

1st Quarter:

Achievements:

1a. Met for half hour with the branch Salesperson, Dispatcher and Manager regarding mix design. Completed by 2/15/94.

1b. Passed quiz on 3/1/94.

3a. Logged total of 10 hours studying maps. Completed on 3/25/94.

3b. Drove alternate routes and compared times. Completed on 3/25/94.

Modifications to Developmental Plan:

None

Date Completed: __4/5/94__

2nd Quarter:

Achievements:

1c. On 7/7/94, reported to Branch Manager one instance of using new mix design knowledge.

2a. Attended Frontline Leadership module on "Dealing with Emotional Behavior" on 6/14/94.

3c. On 5/20/94, demonstrated to Dispatcher the ability to identify quickest,

Modifications to Developmental Plan: safest routes along with good alternatives to three job sites.

Date Completed: __7/20/94__

3rd Quarter:

Achievements:

5a. Completed safety training on 8/10/94 (first opportunity).

2c. On 9/23/94, reported two instances of dealing effectively with two customers who had been unhappy.

Modifications to Developmental Plan:

2b. Night school commitment conflicts with Dale Carnegie course. Course participation postponed until next year.

4a. Unable to leave town for a week. Instead attended seminars at Quarry: "Gradation & Basic Procedures for Aggregates" and "Basic Concrete Technology" completed on 8/3/94. Date Completed: __10/10/94__

This Individual Professional Development Plan is intended to encourage investment in people skills and knowledge growth. It is intended to support your developmental and career objectives. As a development planning and tracking method, it does not assess job performance. rev 1/94

Source: Reprinted with permission of the Granite Rock Company.

career development, learn new skills, achieve job ownership, and be motivated to accept challenge and achieve. In addition, the employees have the authority to design a personal development plan and, in the process, direct the company's investment in their skills and job knowledge, employ their best talents, and feel a sense of accomplishment in building new strengths.

The IPDP process also gives employees a chance to build relationships with others, since many of these plans require coordination and cooperation across departmental boundaries. The process also increases employees' knowledge about the people and jobs throughout the company and helps build strong interpersonal relationships, thus promoting the basis of organizationwide teamwork.

Examining Your Own Organizational Performance

How effectively is your organization evaluating and developing its personnel? In answering this question, respond to each of the following assignments, and ask other members of your management team to do the same. Then compare your answers.

Assignment 1: Answer each of the following by writing your answer directly under the question.

A. What are the key factors you evaluate in your personnel reviews? Identify them and show how they link to your objectives.

| | *Objectives to Which* |
Key Factors Being Reviewed	*They Are Related*

B. Does your organization use peer and/or subordinate reviews of managers? If not, why not? If so, what have you learned as a result of these reviews?

_____

_____

_____

_____

_____

_____

C. Do you track personnel evaluations and future performance? How are the two related? Can you prove this with objective data, as opposed to anecdotal feedback? Explain.

_____

_____

_____

_____

_____

_____

Assignment 2: How is your employee development plan linked to your evaluation process? Be complete in your answer.

_____

_____

_____

_____

_____

_____

_____

_____

A. How do you use your developmental efforts to build a management team that will work efficiently and effectively? Cite two examples.

_____

_____

_____

_____

_____

_____

Wrap-Up

Most organizations agree that people are their most important assets. World-class organizations such as the Baldrige Award winners prove this by carefully evaluating and, even more importantly, developing their associates to bring out the best in each person. The material in this chapter provides some of the basic steps that the companies use in doing this.

One of the most important lessons that you should draw from this chapter was not developed in the material. The lesson is: *Link your evaluations and your developmental plans to your overall objectives.* One of the major problems that IBM faced in the mid- to late 1980s was that many of its personnel had received performance evaluations and developmental assistance designed to help them compete in a market that no longer existed. As a result, the employees were at a disadvantage. They had been trained to think and sell in a mainframe world, but the growth segment of the industry was no longer big iron; it was small iron. As a result, the company had to alter its evaluation and developmental programs and link them to the objectives that were being set in this newly emerging market.

Redirecting personnel efforts can be difficult if the right infrastructure is not in place. In particular, rewards and recognition programs must support and encourage the needed changes. This topic is the focus of Chapter 7.

Chapter 7

Recognize and Reward Accomplishments: Share the Wealth or Grow Poor Together

Many companies find that a carefully designed strategy can help them significantly improve quality, lower costs, and increase market share. In fact, sometimes doing so is not as difficult as management initially anticipates. The challenge, however, is to *maintain* the momentum and stay ahead of the competition— and this is where companies run into trouble. Why? Because they fail to develop the right recognition and infrastructure. After the personnel have achieved the first wave of success, the challenge begins to lose its luster. A feeling of "been there, done that" starts to set in, and organizations eventually return to their old way of doing things. In the process, quality declines, costs rise, and market share shrinks.

The most competitive companies, however, have developed recognition and reward systems that sustain their efforts. Table 7-1 highlights the linkage between performance and quality objectives achieved through performance and recognition systems at AT&T Universal Card Services. While these reward and recognition (R&R) systems take a number of different forms, they typically have the six common characteristics listed on page 165.

Table 7-1. Performance and quality objectives achieved through performance and recognition systems at AT&T Universal Card Systems.

Objective Setting and Performance Appraisal System
(1) Quality and performance measures are established; individual objectives are aligned with corporate and departmental goals; semiannual feedback ensures focus.
(2) Employees and manager together determine objectives and performance standards.

Performance Feedback System
(1) In addition to the manager/employee performance appraisal system, other sources of feedback include matrix management, peer and upward feedback, and matrix management feedback.
(2) Employees provide peer and upward feedback and discuss/review performance results.

Construction Action Plan
(1) Employee performance improvement plan identifies root causes of poor quality and financial performance and formulates countermeasures.
(2) Employee participates in the development of action plan and plan timeline.

Reward/Recognition System
(1) Supports our overall company quality and performance objectives through recognition of significant team and individual contributions. Sharing rallies recognize teams that improve financial and quality performance.
(2) Employee participation (for example, award nominations, award development).

Compensation System
(1) The UCS Excellence Award for managers has three components: achieving daily quality measurements, achieving financial commitments, and contributing an outstanding individual performance. The Associate Excellence Award is based on achieving company quality performance standards daily.
(2) Employee focus groups review compensation system annually. Surveys offer all employees the opportunity to contribute.

Source: Reprinted with permission of AT&T Universal Card Services, 1994.

1. *Visibility.* Those who receive R&R become known to the other in-house personnel and, in many cases, also to the public at large. This is done in a number of ways, such as having the work group's picture appear in the company newsletter along with a story that describes how the team accomplished its results (e.g., significantly reduced cycle time; helped complete an important customer order on time).

2. *Strong customer bias.* R&R is typically given for doing an outstanding job in serving the customer—the person or group that receives the output. This customer can be the in-house personnel who depend on the work group for input or the final customer who receives the ultimate good or service from the group.

3. *Teamwork.* R&R is usually given for teamwork (although individual performance is also rewarded). For example, the company newspaper may announce the names of all team members who helped develop a new consolidated billing system that has cut cycle time by three days.

4. *Identification of results.* R&R systems identify what the group has done and focus praise directly on these efforts. This in turn helps reinforce the company's message: Do a good job and you too will receive recognition and rewards.

5. *Ongoing emphasis.* Every week, month, or quarter, there is an update on what is happening and who is being recognized and rewarded for outstanding results. Organizational personnel are thus continually reinforced for their accomplishments.

6. *Consistency.* All R&R programs are fair and equitable. If all members of a team that reduces the production downtime by 10 percent are given a plaque and a recognition certificate, another team that also reduces production downtime by 10 percent can expect a similar reward. The company does not give the first team the largest reward and give those who follow less than this amount, or the reverse. Rewards are tied to performance in a consistent manner.

In creating and implementing their recognition and reward system, world-class organizations have learned two important lessons that have been of practical value for them. They are:

1. *Develop a system for recognizing all outstanding performance.* There are a number of ways in which this is done, many of which involve nonmonetary rewards. Examples include thank-you notes, plaques, letters of merit, and pins, as well as mention in the in-house newspaper or newsletter. The latter often entails both a story and a picture of the team members who were responsible for performance. These approaches, especially the in-house paper, are often inexpensive ways to keep everyone aware of what is going on in the company and to provide recognition to those who are doing particularly good work.

2. *Create a reward program that is designed especially for your organization.* Recognition is important, but the use of monetary rewards is an important supplement to the process. Typically these rewards are not very large, because companies have found that it is easier and more effective to give small rewards on a continuous basis rather than large rewards on an occasional basis. Examples include quick cash bonuses such as $50 for exemplary work or $100 for a special achievement. Some companies, such as Xerox, also give large salary increases such as 10 to 50 percent of base pay for outstanding performance. However, these rewards are much less common because few people earn them, and the purpose of most R&R programs is to give recognition and rewards to as many people as possible.

The following sections examine how these two lessons are applied by world-class organizations. They are followed by a detailed questionnaire designed to help you evaluate how well your organization is applying these two lessons and to identify areas where improvements need to be made.

Lesson 1: Develop a System for Recognizing All Outstanding Performance

The most competitive companies recognize outstanding performance in a variety of ways. Sometimes recognition is linked to a reward, and the announcement lets everyone know what the person did and how he or she has been honored (e.g., reduced operating costs by 3 percent and was given a check for $250). However, quite often the recognition is nonmonetary and is simply the company's way of letting everyone know that a person or group has done something that warrants attention. The following section examines some recognition programs.

Typical Recognition Programs

One good example of a recognition program is provided by the Ritz-Carlton, where any employee can send a "First Class" card—a 3" × 5" card designed with the company logo—to express his or her appreciation to anyone else in the organization for a job well done. In addition, employees who submit the best ideas for improvement are listed on a bulletin board and given a buffet dinner, and those who generate the greatest number of useful ideas are honored at quarterly receptions.

Another example is provided at Marlow Industries, which maintains a hall of fame and uses service awards, perfect attendance awards, good housekeeping awards, and team recognition awards to call attention to those who are doing outstanding work. Solectron confers the Chairman/CEO Award, which is given for performance, innovation, and invention, and the President's Award, which is given for outstanding quality and customer partnership.

Still another example is provided by Milliken, which is consistently held up as a company that knows how to effectively use recognition as a reward. In every company area, office, and plant there is a display zone that heralds the accomplishments of the personnel who work there. These are sometimes called "alcoves of excellence," and each contains a wide variety of materials, such as displays on recent work improvements, the status of ongoing projects, the name and membership of work teams that are involved in these projects, and plaques, photos, and copies of letters of merit.

Another example of recognition programs is offered by Armstrong Rubber, where there are two levels of recognition: local and corporate. The local effort is managed by quality improvement teams (QITs). The corporate effort takes a number of different forms, including the Awards for Excellence program, which provides individual and team recognition. Everyone is eligible for this award except senior managers, who are recognized through the company's Management Achievement Plan. Another corporatewide program is Team Expo, an international recognition event that Armstrong feels is its most exciting initiative to recognize and reinforce effectiveness of its team-based approach. All QITs are encouraged to participate in the Expo, and those electing to be scored are evaluated by a panel of judges, using the Armstrong Team Universal Measurement System. From 1992 to 1997 more than three hundred teams representing more than 1,000 employees have participated in site Expos, and ten winners (one from each site) participate in the company's finals at Amelia Island, Florida.

Still another example is FedEx, which offers a series of different recognition programs. Three of the most popular are:

1. *Quality pins.* There are three types of quality pins—bronze, silver, and gold. Bronze pins are awarded to groups and teams after they have successfully communicated the results of their problem-solving process to management, either in writing or in presentation format. Silver pins are awarded quarterly to the group or team that submits the best quality success. Gold pins are awarded annually to the team or group that meets the criteria for the silver pin and provides the greatest positive impact on the department, division, or corporation.

2. *Quality seals.* These seals are given by management to show its appreciation and support for quality improvement efforts.

3. *Service Circle of Excellence Award.* This monthly award is given to FedEx stations both domestic and international and is presented for achieving the highest on-time performance during the month.

In addition to giving these rewards, FedEx incorporates quality success stories into its corporate newspaper. The same is true for many other Baldrige Award winners including GTE Directories. The following section examines how this is done.

Use of In-House Newspapers and Newsletters

Quality success stories reported in the company newspaper or newsletter are another form of recognition, and they have been given special attention here because they often offer something that many of the other forms of recognition do not: organization-wide recognition. A person may receive a gold pin or parking for a month in a choice spot near the main entrance. However, many of the honoree's colleagues may not know that the person has received recognition for outstanding performance. In the case of special parking, many companies place the name of the winner on a small sign in front of the spot ("Reserved for This Month's Outstanding Employee: John Brown"). However, even if this is done, many of the employees may not know who John Brown is, so they are unable to personally congratulate him. They simply know the name of the person who has earned the monthly reserved parking spot. In-house newspapers and newsletters overcome this deficiency by focusing on quality success stories.

Increasingly, companies are finding that newsletters and in-house newspapers are an excellent way of ensuring that personnel get the recognition they deserve. Many of the companies that provided information for this book employ such an approach. The following section examines two select companies: Federal Express and GTE Directories.

FedEx World Update

FedEx turns out a magazine entitled *FedEx World Update* that is mailed to all 125,000 employees. There are ten to twelve issues a year, and each issue is approximately forty-eight pages. The contents cover a wide range of topics, including global news briefs, current operational activities, travel, and a review of competitive operations. There is also a section devoted to quality success stories. In each case, the quality story is explained, and the names and pictures of the team members who were responsible for the improvements accompany the story.

GTE Directories *Directions*

GTE Directories produces a monthly newspaper titled *Directions*. The publication is handled by the company's public affairs department and is targeted for employees, their families, and retirees. A typical edition runs sixteen pages, although there is a longer issue every year that focuses heavily on the recognition of award winners companywide. In addition to providing up-to-date information on areas such as company developments (new contracts, new market expansion, corporate sponsorships), industry developments (competitive decisions, industry expansion, Federal Communications Commission decisions), service anniversaries, and region-by-region news, the newspaper highlights success stories of teams that have excelled in the performance of their duties. In Figure 7-1 we provide an example drawn from a recent issue of *Directions*.

Another interesting periodic feature of *Directions* is the request for readers to evaluate the publication and help the editors do an even better job.

Lesson 2: Create a Reward Program That Is Designed Especially for Your Organization

The most competitive American companies have gone about creating a reward program for reinforcing quality-related efforts in a variety of ways. Some of the programs involve promotions or coveted team assignments. In other cases the rewards are monetary and range from a "quick cash" award for doing something exceptional to a bonus for recommending a solution to a job-related problem that results in a cost savings for the organization.

Typical Examples of Reward Systems

At the Ritz-Carlton hotel chain, individuals who consistently meet the organization's performance standards receive verbal and written praise, and high-level performers receive coveted new hotel start-up team assignments. In addition, there are

Figure 7-1. Excerpts from *Directions.*

For One, For All

Community Affairs Administrator Debbie Johnson and Advertising Administrator Silvia Montoya Williams saw a great opportunity for convergence recently when Directories was approached to buy advertising in the 1996 Greater Dallas Chamber of Commerce directory. Working in partnership with colleagues at Telephone Operations and Wireless Services, they developed a specialized ad that features GTE's products and services, including Long Distance, **The Everything Pages®** directory, Wireless Services, and SuperPages℠ interactive services. The ad is featured on the inside front cover of the directory, which has been mailed to 10,000 members of the Greater Dallas Chamber of Commerce. Additionally, the front section of the directory, entitled, "Spotlight on Technology," is distributed to the approximately 20,000 businesses and business leaders who inquire about relocation opportunities in the Dallas area.

Based on the successful initial replacement, the ad has been adapted for other key GTE markets, such as Fort Wayne, Indiana, and Irving, Texas.

East Coast Customer Relations Team

This group exhibits an outstanding attitude and dedication to the goals and spirit of customer service as they each accept an average of nearly 76 inbound calls from Directories' customers each day. While the stated goal for customer relations associates is 10 percent or less abandoned rate and an average speed of answer in 15 seconds or less, this dedicated team averages a speed of answer of 12 seconds (125 percent to goal) and an abandoned rate of only 6.3 percent (158.73 percent to goal).

Congratulations to : Customer Relations Associates Kristine Caccam, Chris Cichon, Ellisa Jordan, Rachele Mitchell, Kristina Mueller, and Ross Smith.

A Lesson in Teamwork

In the spirit of convergence, employees from across the company are banding together to help improve GTE in every way possible. A great example of the growing teamwork between strategic business units (SBUs) includes the recent transfer of GTE Directories' Info Pages production to the National Directory Center (NDC) in Warsaw, Virginia—a change that is saving the company both time and money.

In the past, GTE Telephone Operations was responsible for compiling the Info Pages (the white pages section located at the front of each directory . . .), while GTE Directories employees were responsible for inputting the changes and printing. It was a complicated and lengthy process—often taking three months to complete from start to finish. After conversations between the two SBUs, a group of employees decided to find a better way.

Last spring, a team with representatives from GTE Directories and GTE Telephone Operations was formed under the direction of Ron Roberts, general manager—NDC, and Gary Hruska, assistant vice president—publishing. Their goal? To replace the complicated, paper-intensive procedure handled at five work sites with a simple system managed at one location.

By staying abreast of new technology, the team also learned that the pages could be printed on a low-cost high-resolution plain paper printer (instead of the costly typesetting equipment) and still maintain the company's high printing standards.

Based on the team's suggestions, the NDC staff now makes all of the changes in a single system and gives GTE Directories a final copy ready to print. Implemented ahead of schedule last September, the production has saved the company over $350,000 in the first year alone and now takes just 30 days to complete—meaning customers receive the most up-to-date information possible.

The team was recently recognized for its efforts by both GTE Directories and GTE Telephone Operations. Publishing Systems Training Manager Susan Potter was awarded a Corporate Award of Excellence by GTE Directories for her role in leading the transition, while the entire team was nominated and received an honorable mention for GTE Telephone Operations' President's Leadership Award in the Team Leadership category—the first team with members from another SBU to be nominated for that honor.

"Through their quest to find a better way, this team has helped GTE gain a competitive advantage by significantly streamlining our processes, reducing expenses and maintaining the quality of our directories," notes Hruska. "It's a lesson in teamwork any company would be proud to tell."

Source: Directories, March 1997, p. 11; December 1996, p. 2; and Vol. 4, 1996, p. 2.

team-oriented awards, including bonus pools, which are conferred when recommended solutions are implemented and prove to be effective.

Xerox has a wide array of R&R programs for reinforcing outstanding performance. These include:

Award	Reward
Outstanding Cooperation Award	Medallion
Xerox Achievement Award	$100 to $500
Special Recognition Award	Up to 10 percent of pay
President's Award	Up to 50 percent of pay
Inventory's Award	Patent and money
Salary Supplement	3 to 8 percent of pay
Gain Sharing Programs	Variable monetary reward

FedEx's Reward Program

FedEx uses a number of different approaches to rewarding its personnel. One is tied to its philosophy of promoting from within. A second is its policy of linking pay to performance. A third is its wide array of monetary awards.

Promotion From Within. FedEx stands behind its belief that the people who are now working for the company also represent its future. As a result, the company continually seeks to promote from within, and approximately 75 percent of all job openings are filled with people from the employee ranks. One way FedEx accomplishes this is through its Job Change Tracking System (JCTS), an on-line computer job-posting system that provides most hourly employees with a clear window regarding their advancement path within the organization.

Every Friday the JCTS announces new job openings within the company. If a courier in Maine has her sights on a courier opening in Phoenix, she can enter her name into the JCTS. The system then accesses the company's personnel records and information system in order to retrieve pertinent information on each applicant, including seniority dates, the results of skill and job-knowledge tests, and recent performance evaluations. All employees who seek a posted position receive a numerical score based on job performance and length of service. They are then ranked in order by the system, and at any time during the week after the job is posted the Maine courier can log on to JCTS to see where her name falls on the list of interested applicants. At the end of the week, the individual at the top of the list is awarded the job.

Pay for Performance. At FedEx pay for performance is the rule, not the exception. The company believes that people see a relationship between performance and reward and want to know that when they work extra hard to achieve difficult objectives, their efforts are going to be rewarded. Compensation is tied to the company's three major goals—People, Service, Profit—and this then is translated into a measurable numeric objective.

Hourly employees earn incentive compensation based on performance criteria. Depending on their level of achievement as measured against goals (which include scores achieved on recurrent skill and job-knowledge tests), those employees who have reached the pay limits within their job category can qualify for a "Pro Pay" or individual pay bonus every six months. For first-line and mid-level managers and professionals, incentive compensation is tied to the People-Service-Profit goals through management by objectives (MBO) and by performance-by-objectives (PBO) goal-setting processes (see Figures 7-2 and 7-3). Managers and professionals get points based on their performance as measured against predetermined objectives, and compensation levels, in terms of dollars-per-point, depend on overall company performance as measured against People-Service-Profit (PSP) objectives. While its use of MBO is not revolutionary, FedEx feels that the concept works well within the organization. There are a number of reasons for this.

One reason is that all objectives set through the MBO process are tied to the company's overall PSP objectives. For a regional sales manager, for example, the People goal could be an improvement in leadership performance; the Service goal might specify a certain number of meetings with key customers; the Profit goal might target a particular sales volume. Similarly, for

(Text continues on page 176.)

Figure 7-2. The management by objectives performance statement used at FedEx.

FY Qtr. Name & Number		Department	
Employee Signature Date		Employee Signature Date	
Manager's Signature Date		Manager's Signature Date	
OBJECTIVE (Describe WHAT is to be accomplished, by HOW MUCH or HOW WELL & WHEN)			
ACTION PLAN			
Measurement Method (Describe what constitutes 100% accomplishment of the objective.)			
ACTUAL PERFORMANCE (Description of Achievement)			
TARGET POINTS 1ST 2ND 3RD 4TH		ACTUAL POINTS 1ST 2ND 3RD 4TH	

Source: FedEx.

Figure 7-3. The performance by objectives performance statement used at FedEx.

FY Qtr. Name & Number	Department
Employee Signature Date	Employee Signature Date
Manager's Signature Date	Manager's Signature Date
OBJECTIVE (Describe WHAT is to be accomplished, by HOW MUCH or HOW WELL & WHEN)	
ACTION PLAN	
Measurement Method (Describe what constitutes 100% accomplishment of the objective.)	
ACTUAL PERFORMANCE (Description of Achievement)	
TARGET POINTS 1ST 2ND 3RD 4TH	ACTUAL POINTS 1ST 2ND 3RD 4TH

Source: FedEx.

a line manager the People goal might be development of better listening skills; the Service goal might focus on the completion of two customer-supplier alignments with other departments; and the Profit goal might involve staying within budget. Despite the fact that thousands of individual managers establish personal goals every year, each set of objectives dovetails with those of the manager above the employee and the subordinate below him or her, because all are focused on fundamental corporate objectives and because each employee establishes MBOs or PBOs in close consultation with his or her manager. The result is a cascading effect that ties each level together and directs all levels toward the overall corporate PSP objectives.

A second reason that FedEx's MBO approach to tying rewards and performance works so well is that it has strong top-level involvement. The CEO sets his own objectives each year in conjunction with those of the corporation's board of directors, and from that point on the MBO/PBO process unfolds down and throughout the organization.

A third reason the system works so well is that FedEx has been following the MBO and PBO processes for more than a decade, so the company has been able to work out the rough spots and streamline the system.

A fourth reason, closely tied to the first three, is that FedEx continually analyzes and modifies the system so that it carefully links rewards and performance. In fact, when the company received the Baldrige Award, one of the areas that was cited for excellence was the procedures used to audit and improve the MBO/PBO goal-setting processes.

Monetary Awards. The monetary awards given by FedEx to reinforce quality performance and customer satisfaction are similar to those used by many other organizations. However, FedEx's reward programs have three characteristics:

1. *Decentralization.* Each division controls the performance measurements for the awards to its employees. The company believes that each functional area or division is the best judge of award criteria and the best evaluator of performances that meet and/or exceed these criteria.

2. *Rapid recognition.* Rather than waiting and giving everyone awards at some particular time, such as at an annual awards benefit, the company gives recognition both early and often. Managers are empowered to give "quick cash" bonuses, among other awards, every time they see someone do something that they feel is an outstanding effort and/or that results in the achievement of a deserving outcome.

3. *Customer-driven focus.* The company ties its most prestigious companywide award, the Golden Falcon, directly to complimentary reports from customers. This is done to show clearly the high value that the company assigns to customer satisfaction.

Four of the monetary awards given by FedEx are:

1. *Bravo Zulu (BZ) Award.* The title for this award is borrowed from the U.S. Navy semaphore signal for "well done." The award is given to employees who have exhibited performance above and beyond normal job responsibilities. A BZ can be a monetary or nonmonetary award. The most common BZ is a "quick cash" bonus, typically $50, although the award can take other forms, such as theater tickets or a dinner certificate. These awards are given approximately 2,000 times a month throughout the company, and well over $2 million is disbursed annually.

2. *Five-Star Award.* This award is given to individuals (officers, managing directors, senior manager/managers, individual contributors) whose performance during the fiscal year has exemplified the company quality improvement process philosophy.

3. *Star/Superstar Award.* This award is given to individuals for consistently exceeding their job requirements and for overall performance that clearly places them in the top group of employees. This award provides a percentage of the employee's salary as a lump sum cash award.

4. *Golden Falcon/Humanitarian Award.* This, the highest honor, is given to nonmanagement employees who demonstrate exceptional performance achievements or unselfish acts that enhance customer service or who promote human welfare above

and beyond community responsibility. Each Golden Falcon award includes ten shares of stock and a congratulatory phone call or visit from the company's chief operating officer and is triggered by a letter or phone call from either the person's manager or a customer in praise of a FedEx employee's above-and-beyond-the-call-of-duty performance.

Zytec's Approach

The Zytec Corporation, a Baldrige Award winner, has developed a recognition program that is tied directly to its implemented improvement system. The Implemented Improvement System (IIS) is a Japanese-style suggestion system that places major emphasis on employee involvement with the goal of generating new ideas for increased productivity. There are three stages to IIS. During the first stage, the organization encourages employees to examine their jobs and work areas, think of ways of improving them, and make small improvements; in the second stage, the organization develops and educates employees so that they are better equipped to analyze problems, devise ideal solutions, and undertake more ambitious improvements; in the third stage, the organization encourages employees to pursue major improvements so that significant benefits can be realized.

Zytec combines this IIS program with a recognition system that is specifically designed to reinforce new ideas and improvements. The system works this way:

1. For each idea an employee submits, he or she receives a $1 token cash award plus a lottery ticket, which is presented at his or her work station.

2. The work group with the highest percentage of employee participation (typically everyone in the group has submitted at least one idea) gets to display a trophy for a month, after which it is presented to another group.

3. Each month the names of all employees participating in the program are put in a hat, and one name is drawn for a day off with pay.

4. The winner of the day off with pay chooses a support or staff person to take over his or her job for one day.

5. Each month the program administrator asks for a volunteer from each work group to serve on the review board, which examines all ideas submitted that month and chooses the top three. The employees who submitted the top three ideas are given $100, $75, and $50, respectively.

6. Each month the program administrator takes pictures of the three winners and places them on the bulletin boards.

7. A copy of the review board's minutes is published in the company newsletter each month.

In addition, Zytec folds this monetary reward system into an overall recognition system via the monthly newsletter, which includes explanations of each winning idea in an effort to trigger more ideas from employees and provides information on two important ways that employees can reward each other. One is through the use of the Zystroke form (see Chapter 2); the other is by the use of a "warm fuzzy," a bead or certificate that serves as a personal thank-you. Figure 7-4 shows the number of warm fuzzies and Zystrokes that were given out at Zytec during the first months of a recent year.

Examining Your Own Organizational Performance

Does your organization recognize and reward accomplishments? How satisfied are the personnel with the R&R system? Are you continually revising and updating these approaches on the basis of evaluation and feedback? In answering these questions in more depth, read and respond to the assignment and ask other members of your management team to do the same. When you are finished, compare and analyze your answers.

Assignment: In drawing together all of the ideas and lessons in this chapter, complete the evaluation questionnaire that starts on page 181 by rating your organization on a scale of 1 to 10. Use the descriptions to help guide your ranking choice. When you are finished, total your points and read the interpretation of the score.

Figure 7-4. "Warm fuzzies" and Zystrokes (a recent five-month tally).

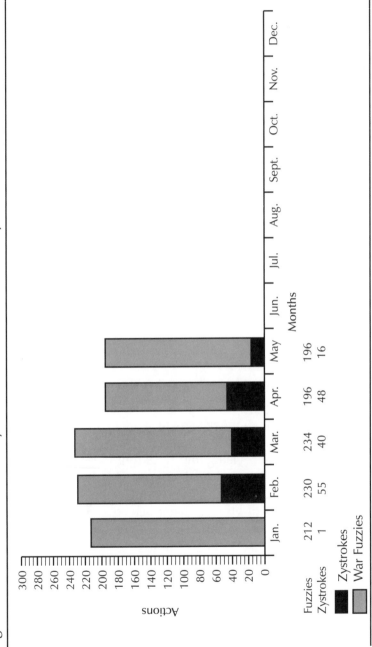

	Jan.	Feb.	Mar.	Apr.	May
Fuzzies	212	230	234	196	196
Zystrokes	1	55	40	48	16

■ Zystrokes
▨ War Fuzzies

Source: Reprinted with permission of the Zytec Corporation.

1. Aside from salaries, what types of rewards does your organization give to the personnel?

				Infrequent but large financial rewards		Frequent small and infrequent large financial rewards			Frequent small and infrequent large financial rewards, as well as formal recognition in the employee's unit or department
None									
0	1	2	3	4	5	6	7	8	9	10

2. Which of the following best describes your organization's R&R programs?

They are a blend of financial rewards coupled with recognition and praise from both management and one's peer group		They are mostly financial, with some recognition and praise from management		They are totally focused on financial rewards		We don't have any
10	9	8	7	6	5	4	3	2	1	0

3. How closely are rewards tied to the organization's overall goals?

There is little linkage		There is some linkage		There is a great deal of linkage		There is total linkage
0	1	2	3	4	5	6	7	8	9	10

4. How closely are recognition and rewards tied to both internal and external customer service?

	Totally			A great deal		Very little		None	
10	9	8	7	6	5	4	3	2	1	0

5. What does the reward system promote?

Neither individual effort nor teamwork		A small amount of both individual effort and teamwork		A fair degree of both individual effort and teamwork		A great degree of both individual effort and teamwork			
0	1	2	3	4	5	6	7	8	9	10

6. Over the past three years, what percent of personnel have received recognition and/or rewards?

	90–100 percent			75–89 percent		50–74 percent		Less than 50 percent	
10	9	8	7	6	5	4	3	2	1	0

7. What percent of personnel are eligible for recognition and rewards?

	Less than 25 percent			About half		Most of the personnel		Everyone	
0	1	2	3	4	5	6	7	8	9	10

8. Judging from feedback from associates, how fair and equitable is the R&R program?

	Associates feel that it is totally fair and equitable			Most feedback is highly positive		Feedback is mixed but more positive than negative		Most feedback is negative	
10	9	8	7	6	5	4	3	2	1	0

9. Is it clear to the organizational personnel why individuals and teams are given recognition and rewards?

				They have some knowledge			They almost always know			It is totally clear to them
	No									
0	1	2	3	4	5	6	7	8	9	10

10. Are organizational personnel aware of who is being recognized and rewarded for outstanding performance?

They are fully aware				They have a pretty good idea			They are somewhat knowledgeable			They have no idea
10	9	8	7	6	5	4	3	2	1	0

11. Does the organization have a formal system for communicating quality success stories?

				Yes, but it doesn't work very well			Yes, and it is getting better all the time			Yes, and it works extremely well
	No									
0	1	2	3	4	5	6	7	8	9	10

12. How often does the organization's R&R system allow for rewards for outstanding performance?

Virtually every day				Often			Seldom			Never
10	9	8	7	6	5	4	3	2	1	0

13. How often does the organization recognize and reward outstanding performance?

							Outstanding performance is recognized on a quarterly basis			Recognition and rewards are given on a daily/ weekly basis
	There is no R&R program			There is an annual awards program						
0	1	2	3	4	5	6	7	8	9	10

14. How actively involved is top management in supporting the R&R system?

	Totally			A great deal		A little bit			Not at all	
10	9	8	7	6	5	4	3	2	1	0

15. Who has input regarding the design and operation of the R&R system?

	Top management only			A formal R&R committee			Representatives from every management level			Representatives from all organizational levels
0	1	2	3	4	5	6	7	8	9	10

16. How often is the R&R system reviewed?

	On an ongoing basis			Every couple of years			When things seem to be going wrong			Never	
10	9	8	7	6	5	4	3	2	1	0

17. Is there a formal committee or group that is responsible for reviewing and modifying the R&R system?

	No			Yes, but it doesn't really do very much			Yes, and it does a pretty good job			Yes, and it's active and responsive to changing conditions
0	1	2	3	4	5	6	7	8	9	10

18. Is there an informal R&R system that has sprung up within the organization?

Yes, and it exists throughout the organization				Yes, in most departments			Only in a small number of departments			No	
10	9	8	7	6	5	4	3	2	1	0

19. How often is feedback solicited from the personnel regarding the effectiveness of the R&R program?

	Never			Seldom			Often			Continually
0	1	2	3	4	5	6	7	8	9	10

20. How satisfied are the personnel with the current R&R program?

				A great deal			Somewhat			Not at all
	Totally									
10	9	8	7	6	5	4	3	2	1	0

Instructions: Total all of your response scores, and compare your score to the interpretation key below:

Interpretation Key

200–240 points — Your organization is doing an excellent job with its R&R program, but some fine tuning might help even more.

160–199 points — Your organization needs to identify those areas with a score of 7 or less and look for ways of improving its R&R program in each case.

120–159 points — Your organization needs to carefully review its overall R&R program, especially in those areas with scores of 6 or less, and make significant changes designed to improve responses/results in each of these areas.

120 points — Your organization needs to radically rethink and redesign its R&R program by using these questions to help guide and focus its efforts.

Wrap-Up

The questionnaire in the preceding section can be particularly helpful in pinpointing those areas where your R&R program needs to be improved. The most important thing to keep in mind when modifying or redesigning the system is that the key to an effective R&R program is feedback.

There are a number of ways of providing feedback. One is

by encouraging the personnel to offer suggestions for modifications or additions to the present system. Another, and supplemental, way is to continually track the value of the reward and recognition system and note which approaches are working well, which are losing their effectiveness, and which are no longer of any value. The most difficult challenge is to determine how the efficacy of each element of the R&R system can be tracked. Fortunately, customer feedback (both internal and external) can be extremely useful in this process. So can careful evaluation of other quantitative measures that are directly related to performance results.

These efforts can also be useful in maintaining the overall quality emphasis and ensuring that the momentum is not lost. One way in which this is done is through carefully designed continuous improvement efforts. This is the focus of attention in Chapter 8.

Chapter 8

Keep On Going:
You're Only as Good as
Last Quarter's Performance

Today on Wall Street a company's latest sales figures can cause the company's stock to race ahead or drop back sharply, depending on the nature of the news. Similarly, organizations that announce they are downsizing and laying off 1,000 workers are likely to find their shares pushed ever higher by investors who are certain that this strategy will produce rapid and long-lasting bottom-line results. Simply put, a growing number of people are now placing an inordinate amount of faith in short-term results, so companies that are interested in improving their quality and widening their customer bases must keep in mind that short-term performance can sometimes be as important as long-run results.

There are a number of ways that this short-term/long-term focus can be maintained. These include consideration of innovative processes, the development of effective benchmarking techniques, and the creation of an ongoing continuous improvement system. All three are examined in this chapter. In addition, we consider some of the ideas that were developed in Chapter 1, notably, the importance of rejecting popular myths regarding how to improve quality and performance and, instead, focusing on data-based findings. In carrying out these steps, Baldrige Award winners rely heavily on two lessons:

1. *Look for ways to innovate the current work processes and procedures.* The largest increases in quality and productivity are often the result of significantly innovative approaches. This does not mean that organizations abandon their interest in incremental improvements but rather that they complement this idea of "thinking small" with a willingness to "think big." This idea is becoming particularly popular in Japan, where many world-class organizations are coming to believe that incremental improvements alone are not sufficient to allow them to maintain their world-class status.

2. *Develop an effective benchmarking and continuous improvement system that relies on New-Age thinking.* In both innovating and achieving incremental improvements, benchmarking is particularly important because it provides the basis for doing things differently and often provides the organization with an opportunity to think outside the box. Meanwhile, continuous improvement helps enterprises squeeze more profit and productivity out of their current processes and procedures. Yet both these approaches will prove fruitless if management does not continually review its thinking and ensure that its view of quality and productivity is based on facts and not merely on intuition and anecdotal information. This idea was developed in Chapter 1 and is revisited at the end of this chapter.

The following sections examine how some of the companies studied in this book use these two lessons to compete effectively. After you have finished reading these lessons, the last section of the chapter provides you the opportunity to apply them to your organization.

Lesson 1: Look for Ways to Innovate the Current Work Processes and Procedures

One of the ways in which Baldrige Award winners continue improving the quality of their goods and services is through innovative processes. Innovation involves dramatic improvements in productivity and is likely to be attained only intermittently, in contrast to typical continuous improvement efforts that focus on achieving small, incremental, and continuous gains. However, when innovation is achieved, the gains are significant—and there are a number of ways that Baldrige Award companies have used innovation to improve quality.

Eastman Chemical, for example, encourages innovation by providing a structured way of linking ideas for new products with its corporate business plans. Through the use of the "Eastman Innovation Process," teams of employees from various areas such as business, sales, research, engineering, and manufacturing shepherd a product idea from inception to market. Early in this process, customer needs are considered and then validated and revalidated. As a result of these approaches, the time to bring a new product to market has been reduced by 50 percent in recent years, and the company averages 22 percent of sales from new products that have been commercialized within the past five years.

Another example of innovation in action is provided by Universal Card Services, which links its innovation process to empowerment, thus freeing associates to assume responsibility, take risks, and develop creative solutions that will delight the customer. Innovation is also supported through specific programs such as: (1) "Your Ideas . . . Your Universe," which encourages employees to submit quality improvement ideas; (2) the monthly marketing program review, which shares program goals and results and provides a basis for improvement ideas; and (3) the monthly marketing data review, which shares customer feedback and is used to generate new ideas and improvement opportunities for all employees.

Other examples are Granite Rock's "TransloadXpress" and "GraniteXpress" systems for loading and unloading railroad cars and for handling customer deliveries. These approaches were developed specifically to help the company increase productivity and improve customer service.

Granite Rock's "TransloadXpress" and "GraniteXpress"

Granite Rock has developed highly creative approaches for unloading materials from bulk commodity rail cars and for filling customer orders. But approaches have required the company to create special equipment that has revolutionized the way these jobs are done.

Transload Technology

One of the most time-consuming chores facing Granite Rock is the loading and unloading of bulk commodity rail cars. In response, the company created its own technology for handling the work. The company calls its system the "TransloadXpress" because of the speed with which this mobile conveyor system can load and unload commodities. At the heart of the process is a specially designed truck with a long conveyor belt that can be rotated 360 degrees and raised or lowered as needed to pick up or deposit materials. This conveyor belt can also be automatically unfolded and stretched out so that it extends from the mobile conveyor system in both directions. This allows materials to be placed on one end of the conveyor and dropped off at the other end. For example, if the TransloadXpress unit is being used to pick up materials from a rail car, one end of the conveyor belt can be stretched out and lowered beneath the rail car and the other end positioned over the pickup vehicle that will be receiving the materials. Using a hydraulic piston to control the optimal discharge of material, the system can then begin unloading the rail car, transporting the materials from one end of the conveyor belt to the other—and this can all be done by a single operator who sets up the entire system. The process also works the other way. For example, materials can be moved from an end-dump truck to the conveyor belt and carried down to a rail car.

The TransloadXpress is engineered to convey materials at rates up to eight hundred tons per hour, with rail-to-truck rates averaging three hundred tons per hour. In addition, when the cost of transporting materials by truck is compared to that of combining TransloadXpress with rail, the company estimates that overall transportation costs can be reduced by up to 50 percent, because of the reduction in both truck road miles and total miles.

A simple case study illustrates the benefits of the Transload-Xpress. Assume a construction project requires ten thousand tons of aggregate. The site is one hundred miles from the optimal quarry, and there is a rail spur five miles from the job site.

Trucking	*Rail*
400 truckloads (25 tons/truck)	100 hopper cars (20,000 rail miles, 4,000 truck road miles)
Total: 80,000 truck road miles (round-trip)	Total: 24,000 rail/truck miles (round-trip)

GraniteXpress Loadout System

Another innovative feature of Granite Rock's operation is its method for loading materials for clients. This express system is designed to simplify the process of picking up materials, thus allowing customers to get back to their own job sites in record time. While the process involves a series of steps, the following description provides an overview.

1. When a customer drives into the quarry to pick up materials, the individual pulls on to twin scales and holds his or her GraniteXpress card up to a card reader. The individual then tells the weighmaster whom he or she is hauling for, the products wanted, the tonnage in each trailer, and the job to which the materials will be hauled. The weighmaster then assigns the individual to a loadout lane.

2. The driver then goes to the assigned lane, and the order is displayed on a screen so that the individual can verify its accuracy. After ensuring that the truck is correctly positioned to receive the materials, the driver gives a pull cord two long, steady pulls, and the materials are discharged. When a green light signals that the order is complete, the driver proceeds to the weighout station at the scalehouse.

3. The individual is then given a sales tag, which he or she uses to verify that the order has been properly filled. The driver

then signs and removes the top copy for the weighmaster and keeps the back-up copy as a receipt.

This system is simple and quick and enables Granite Rock to handle a large number of customers every day. The success of the system can be tied directly to the company's ability to innovate the work flow and to create a process for automating the way in which materials are loaded. As a result, the company is one of the most productive in the industry.

Lesson 2: Develop an Effective Benchmarking and Continuous Improvement System That Relies on New-Age Thinking

The basis for a great deal of innovation by Baldrige Award winners can be found in benchmarking and continuous improvement efforts. The following discussion examines ways that these processes are employed.

Benchmarking Efforts

Benchmarking is an ongoing process of measuring one company's products, services, and practices against those of competitors or organizations that are recognized as industry leaders.

Process and Applications

The general steps in the benchmarking process do not vary much from organization to organization. Xerox employs ten steps, as shown in Figure 8-1, and these, in one version or another, are followed by just about every organization that uses the process.

Overall, there are four different types of benchmarking: internal, competitive, functional, and generic. Texas Instruments notes that each of these contributes to improvements but that some are more important than others, as shown in the table that follows Figure 8-1.

Figure 8-1. Xerox benchmarking process.

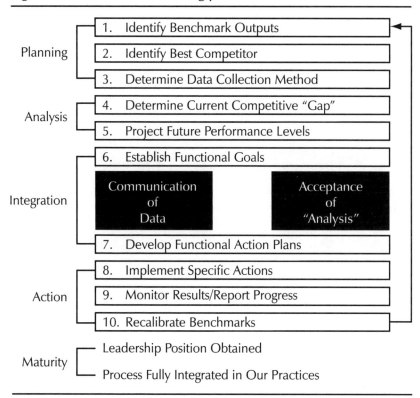

Planning	1. Identify Benchmark Outputs
	2. Identify Best Competitor
	3. Determine Data Collection Method
Analysis	4. Determine Current Competitive "Gap"
	5. Project Future Performance Levels
Integration	6. Establish Functional Goals
	Communication of Data Acceptance of "Analysis"
	7. Develop Functional Action Plans
Action	8. Implement Specific Actions
	9. Monitor Results/Report Progress
	10. Recalibrate Benchmarks
Maturity	Leadership Position Obtained
	Process Fully Integrated in Our Practices

Source: Reprinted with permission of Xerox Corporation, 1996.

Type of Benchmarking	Activity Performed	Amount of Improvement
Internal	Compare similar processes within the company	10%
Competitive	Make specific competitor-to-competitor comparisons	20%
Functional	Compare specific functions to similar functions at industry leaders	35%
Generic	Compare unrelated practices or processes	>35%

Xerox breaks the benchmarking process into three activities: observe, understand, and act. In each case, key questions or functions are carried out. Here is a thumbnail sketch of how it works:

In carrying out this activity:	*These questions are answered or steps taken:*
Observe	► Who's best? ► How do you know? ► Can you identify their practices?
Understand	► Are others better at this job or process? ► Why are they better? ► How much better? ► What do they do that can be adopted by us?
Act	► A commitment is made to setting goals. ► This new direction is communicated to everyone who needs to know this information. ► Action to introduce the changes associated with these new goals is undertaken. ► On the basis of the decisions and actions, benchmarks are recalibrated.

Benchmarking has been particularly useful in helping Baldrige Award organizations reduce their error rates and drive up quality-related factors such as customer satisfaction and "time to market." For example, Ames Rubber has used the process to reduce the defect rate for its largest customer, Xerox, from more than 30,000 parts per million (ppm) to eleven. As a result, Ames is now the "benchmark" producer of fuser rollers for the very highest speed copiers. At the same time, delivery performance for Ames' top customers is well above the industry average, and productivity, as measured by sales per teammate, has increased sharply.

Another example of benchmarking is provided by GTE Directories, which uses a host of different information sources to help it carry out benchmarking activities. These include industry comparison data, customer satisfaction feedback, internal and external competitive analysis of both products and services, information from other GTE business units for business and support services as well as employee and supplier performance data, and industry studies for operation and support services benchmarks. The company uses these data to compare its current processes to those of other world-class companies and then sets and validates world-class targets of its own. Using these processes, the company's Leadership Council then determines gaps and identifies the quality improvement opportunities that can have the greatest impact on customer satisfaction. In addition, the company continually provides process management tools and training to its people, empowering them to make ongoing assessment of opportunities for quality improvement and to take appropriate action. In fact, benchmarking is the primary vehicle used for information gathering and analysis, and in refining these efforts GTE Directories has reduced the number of steps in its own benchmarking process from eleven to six.

Motorola's Approach to Benchmarking

While Xerox is best known for its pioneering work in benchmarking, Motorola has been extremely successful in both refining the process and applying it to myriad activities. In particular, Motorola closely links its benchmarking efforts to its six-sigma program. It does so by defining those factors that it judges critical to long-term success and then comparing its performance in these areas to that of the competition and/or best-in-class performers. This information is then used to develop business strategies and functional plans. In doing so, Motorola relies on a five-step process (see Figure 8-2) that entails consideration of both internal and external data. These steps include:

Figure 8-2. Motorola's five-step benchmarking plan.

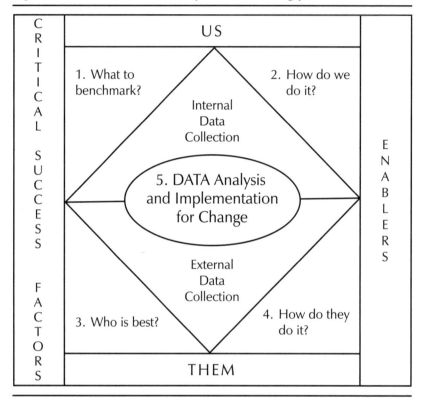

Source: Motorola Corporation.

1. The topics that are to be benchmarked are identified.
2. The approach to be used for gathering data is determined.
3. Benchmarking partners who are the best in terms of the functions and processes being studied are identified, and a partnering agreement is formulated for the mutual exchange of information.
4. The benchmarking partner's approach is carefully studied in order to answer two questions: What enables them to be the best? How do they do it?

5. An action plan is created for both analyzing the data and implementing follow-on action.

Steps 1 and 3 in Figure 8-2 (left side of the diagram) represent the critical success factors—and these are often the most difficult to determine. In identifying them, some of the most commonly asked questions are:

➤ How much do we know about our company's critical success?
➤ What do our customers buy from us?
➤ What makes our company what it is?
➤ Why would our customers recommend our services?

The answers help highlight critical success factors and link them to the strategic plan. This activity also helps identify gaps that exist between the company's current and desired performance.

In drawing all of this together, Motorola uses a five-phase process, which is depicted in Figure 8-3. By measuring input and output at every point, Motorola is able to pinpoint results and hold people accountable for their activities and actions. As noted in Chapter 2, Motorola firmly believes that "what you measure is what you get."

Motorola also points out that its approach is useful in promoting renewal because it focuses on identifying and correcting errors and getting the personnel committed to doing things the new way. By creating a culture of change that is committed to continually finding better ways of doing things, the company is able to link its benchmarking efforts and six sigma into a strategy that results in best-in-class performance. A good example is the way in which it reduced cycle time for financial closings. In the late 1980s this activity was being performed at approximately a three-sigma level. Today financial closing activities are world-class and benchmarked by others. Here is a historical look at how these efforts helped Motorola reach this new level of excellence:

Figure 8-3. Inputs and outputs in Motorola's benchmarking process.

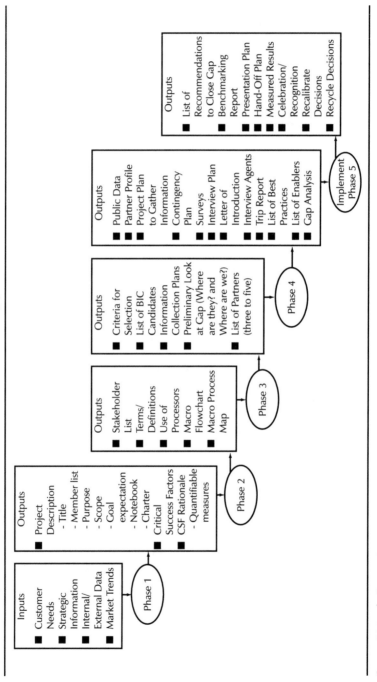

Source: Motorola Corporation.

Year and Sigma Level	*Time Required for Closing*
1987 closing— approximately 3 sigma	9 days
April 1990 closing— approximately 5 sigma	4 days
June 1992 closing— approximately 6 sigma	2 days
Current performance by some units—6 sigma	1 day
Current objective for all units—6 + sigma	On demand from client

Pillars, Metrics, and Spider Diagrams

Another approach that is beginning to gain popularity among world-class companies is the use of pillars, metrics, and spider diagrams. What makes this approach particularly useful is that it allows the company to focus on a host of areas that are critical to success, measure and plot performance in each of these areas, and then make an overall evaluation of the organization's world-class performance standing.

Identifying the Pillars. Pillars are the key factors or bases that help determine the enterprise's ability to compete effectively. Depending on the specific organization, the number of pillars can vary widely. Common examples of pillars include customer focus, resources and capabilities, strategic vision, value creation, and quality focus. In each case the organization defines the nature and scope of the pillar. Here is how this could be done for the five pillars that were just noted:

- ► *Customer focus*—the ability to identify, anticipate, and respond to internal and external customer needs both now and in the future
- ► *Resources and capabilities*—the assets and talents with which the organization creates value for the customer, including technologies, facilities, and organizational climate

➤ *Strategic vision*—the mental view of the type of organization that senior-level management would like the enterprise to become
➤ *Value creation*—the ability to produce or increase benefits perceived by customers so that they feel they are getting more value than they expected or previously received
➤ *Quality focus*—the ability to provide state-of-the-art output that is at least as good as that of the competition and that results in customers identifying the company as a high-quality producer

These pillars all have characteristics that serve as the basis for measurement. Table 8-1 provides a partial list of some of the characteristics associated with them. Using these characteristics as a point of departure, metrics are then developed for each pillar.

Determining the Metrics. Metrics are standards used for measuring each of the characteristics. In order to make this task somewhat easier to carry out, it is common for an organization to appoint a committee that is familiar with the work and to charge the group with developing the appropriate set of metrics.

In some cases a pillar has two or three metrics that collectively determine performance in that area. In other cases the pillar may have as many as a dozen metrics that are measured in arriving at a global evaluation of that pillar. A total of twenty-five characteristics are listed in Table 8-1; an organization using these would create a metric for each. One of the main questions in creating a metric is: How many degrees of measurement should we use in a metric? Typically there are four or five. Fewer than this produces results that are too general. For example, consider a metric with three degrees: poor, adequate, and excellent. If a company is performing better than adequately but does not feel it is excellent on this pillar, what metric score should it assign? On the other hand, if the metric has six or more degrees, this can result in the committee splitting hairs, for example, between "poor" and "below average" or between "above average" and "good." One way of avoiding these problems is to limit the number of degrees being measured and then define each of them in detail. In Tables 8-2 and 8-3, we provide examples by

Table 8-1. Characteristics of pillars (a partial example).

Pillar	Key Characteristics
Customer focus	Customer satisfaction Customer involvement Market diversification
Resources and capabilities	Personnel quality Budget Research, development, and engineering capabilities, skills, and talents Use of external resources Important technologies Organizational climate Information technology Facilities and infrastructure
Strategic vision	Alignment of vision and mission Anticipatory strategy planning Stakeholder buy-in Leadership
Value creation	Proper portfolio Product performance Cycle time and responsiveness Value of work in progress
Quality focus	Capacity for breakthroughs Continuous improvement Commitment to quality Structured processes Learning environment Quality of research

choosing two of the twenty-five characteristics that were identified in Table 8-1 and presenting a metric for each that describes four degrees of performance or output.

Creating a Spiderweb. The last step in this process is to create a spiderweb diagram that gives an overall picture of how well

(Text continues on page 204.)

Table 8-2. Example of an "important technologies" metric for a resources and capabilities pillar in a research, development, and engineering (RD&E) center.

Characteristic	Performance Level	Metric
Important technologies	Poor	There are no systematic programs or processes for introducing, managing, or assessing research technologies in the research program.
	Adequate	Base technologies being developed for use in the research program are necessary for fulfilling technological needs but offer little differentiation in product performance from other alternatives; important technologies are recognized, developed, and used, but technology development is not advanced.
	Good	Pacing technologies are being developed or used in the research program; these technologies have the potential to change significantly the nature of the research program, but they are not yet embodied in products; incorporation of pacing technologies results in leap ahead developments.
	Excellent	RD&E programs are anticipatory; development and incorporation of new technology to support RD&E and product development are planned and adequately funded; new areas of research and technology are appreciated, and researchers understand the implications of particular research programs; new scientific discoveries are frequently translated into pacing technologies within the organization.

Table 8-3. Example of a "leadership" metric for a strategic vision pillar in a research, development, and engineering (RD&E) center.

Characteristic	Performance Level	Metric
Leadership	Poor	Commitment of senior leadership to the strategic vision or research plan is poorly communicated to the staff; administrative and product development managers are not involved in planning the direction of future research or developing the business plan; personnel are suspicious or do not trust the organization's leadership; stakeholders view the senior leadership as ineffectual and reactive.
	Adequate	The strategic vision and research plan are understood by the staff; resources (i.e., time, personnel, and dollars) are aligned to meet these plans; the staff trusts senior leadership and is receptive to new ideas and re-engineering opportunities.
	Good	Management and staff codevelop plans that are understood and embraced by staff and stakeholders alike; ideas flow freely and in both directions between management and staff.
	Excellent	The leadership has created an air of excitement and commitment throughout the entire laboratory; bold and creative ideas are encouraged and funded; RD&E successes are rapidly exploited, and ideas are rewarded; failure is considered an opportunity to learn.

the organization is doing vis-à-vis world-class organizations or other companies against which the organization is benchmarking itself. This typically is done in two steps. First, the committee charged with the assignment constructs an organizational assessment table that incorporates all of the characteristics that were measured for each pillar. (See Table 8-4 for an example.) After these individual evaluations are completed, a decision is made regarding an overall assessment for that pillar. For example, in the case of the customer focus pillar in Table 8-4, there are three characteristics. If all three are evaluated as "good," then the pillar assessment will be good. However, if there is a split vote, such as four for "adequate" and three for "good," the committee might give an overall assessment of "adequate." In some cases the members do not vote for one of the four assessment choices but rather select an in-between choice, for example, by placing an "X" between "adequate" and "good." When there are a series of these in-between choices for pillar characteristics, the committee often uses a combination of quantitative and qualitative judgments in arriving at an overall assessment.

When all of the pillar assessments have been completed, the group then places the results on a spider diagram. An example is provided in Figure 8-4. In this example, five pillars have been developed for evaluation purposes, so the spider diagram is pentagonal in shape. Each of the five points of the pentagon represents one of the pillars and is labeled accordingly. In addition, in each case a four-point scale emanates from the origin of the diagram to the pentagonal point. This scale is the metric and is used to record the overall ranking that the committee gave to the particular pillar. In the hypothetical case reported in Figure 8-4, the organizational unit that was evaluated received a score of just under 3 for customer focus; a score between 1 and 2 for strategic vision; a score of 2 for value creation; a score of approximately 2.5 for quality focus; and a score around 3.5 for resources and capability. These scores are all based on the assumption that the best organization against which the unit is being benchmarked would have received a rating of 4.

This information is then entered in the spider diagram, and the points are connected with straight lines. As shown in Figure 8-4, this results in a small, lopsided pentagon within the larger,

Table 8-4. An overall assessment score sheet for performance on
the characteristics of world-class pillars for an RD&E organization.

Pillars/Characteristics	Assessment			
	Poor	Adequate	Good	Excellent
Customer Focus Pillar				
Customer satisfaction	‎	‎	‎	‎
Customer involvement	‎	‎	‎	‎
Market diversification	‎	‎	‎	‎
Pillar assessment	‎	‎	‎	‎
Resources and Capabilities Pillar				
Personnel quality	‎	‎	‎	‎
Budget	‎	‎	‎	‎
RD&E capabilities, skills, talents	‎	‎	‎	‎
Use of external resources	‎	‎	‎	‎
Important technologies	‎	‎	‎	‎
Organizational climate	‎	‎	‎	‎
Information technology	‎	‎	‎	‎
Facilities and infrastructure	‎	‎	‎	‎
Pillar assessment	‎	‎	‎	‎
Strategic Vision Pillar				
Alignment of vision and mission	‎	‎	‎	‎
Anticipatory strategic planning	‎	‎	‎	‎
Stakeholder buy-in	‎	‎	‎	‎
Leadership	‎	‎	‎	‎
Pillar assessment	‎	‎	‎	‎
Value Creation Pillar				
Proper portfolio	‎	‎	‎	‎
Product performance	‎	‎	‎	‎
Cycle time and responsiveness	‎	‎	‎	‎
Value of work in progress	‎	‎	‎	‎
Pillar assessment	‎	‎	‎	‎
Quality Focus Pillar				
Capacity for breakthroughs	‎	‎	‎	‎
Continuous improvement	‎	‎	‎	‎
Commitment to quality	‎	‎	‎	‎
Structured processes	‎	‎	‎	‎
Learning environment	‎	‎	‎	‎
Quality of research	‎	‎	‎	‎
Pillar assessment	‎	‎	‎	‎

Figure 8-4. A spiderweb diagram for measuring performance against world-class competitors.

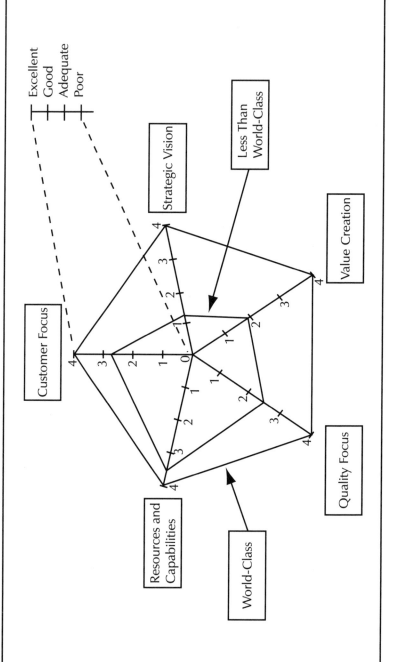

symmetrical pentagon. The inner spider diagram shows how well the unit compares to world-class organizations on each of the five pillars.

The results in Figure 8-4 appear to indicate that the unit is not doing well. However, this is not necessarily true. Each of the five outer points on the pentagon represents the best performance by the company that is being benchmarked. However, it is not necessary to be world-class on every pillar in order to be a world-class organization. In fact, most companies that are benchmarked are world leaders in one pillar but not in others. So the benchmarking company may be looking at a host of different organizations when it benchmarks itself on the basis of world-class pillars.

The primary benefit of the type of analysis provided in Figure 8-4 is that it helps the benchmarking company identify where its performance gaps are greatest vis-à-vis world-class enterprises. Quite often a world-class company is excellent on one or two of the five pillars and good on the remaining three. This provides the unit with a basis for its continuous improvement efforts.

Continuous Improvement in Action

Closely linked to benchmarking efforts is continuous improvement (CI)—and there are a variety of ways in which Baldrige Award winners strive to maintain their CI efforts. One of the most common methods is monitoring operational results such as error rates and customer satisfaction feedback. Another is focusing on indirect measures such as the percentage of payroll that is allocated for training. The logic behind this strategy is that if more money is spent on well-designed training, the results are bound to be reflected on the bottom line. A good example is Wainwright Industries, which currently spends 7 percent of its payroll for training and believes that this is why it has been able to significantly increase its customer satisfaction levels as well as drive up the number of implementable suggestions by associates.

AT&T Consumer Communications Services collects key types of data that support quality improvement in a number of critical areas. In Table 8-5 we detail how the organization does this. A close examination of this table shows that CI is pursued in a wide variety of areas, including customer focus, product and service performance, and financial results.

Six Sigma Revisited

Before concluding the discussion of CI, it is important to note that many of the concepts discussed earlier in the book play a key role in helping ensure continuous progress. Six sigma is an excellent example, because it forces companies to set quantifiable targets that can be used to measure performance objectively and direct future action.

Another reason that programs such as six sigma are important is that they help prevent organizations from becoming complacent and falling into erroneous thinking. In Chapter 1 some of the common erroneous concepts that are held by many organizations were highlighted as myths and then debunked. One of these myths warrants additional consideration: the belief that increased quality, especially at the six-sigma level (3.4 defects per million) costs far more than it generates. Quality assurance people at Motorola note that this thinking is fallacious. One of them put it this way:

> Consider these facts and analysis. A product with 10,000 parts or processes, each of which is one hundred PPM [parts per million] defective, will contain an average of one defect per unit. In fact, only 36.79% of the units will go through the entire process without a defect. Out of every 1,000 units made, 632 will have to be repaired at least once. Of these, 368 units will have one repair, 184 will have two repairs, sixty-one will have three, fifteen will have four, three will have five, and one will need six repairs.

So it is important to have robust designs that reduce the opportunities for defects to creep into the final product. This is a one-time expense. If it is not done, however, the cost of repairs will continue throughout the life of the product! Moreover, even

Table 8-5. Data collection and continuous quality improvement.

Examples of Key Types of Data	Supports Quality Improvement in:
Customer related	
Customer satisfaction	Customer-contact associate (CCA) performance, service delivery, customer requirement definition, retention
Customer needs assessment/data	Forecasting customer requirements, designing new/enhanced products/ services, targeting products/services to market segments, assessing process effectiveness
Product and service performance	
Network servicing	Conformance to customer requirements, determining network enhancements
Customer servicing	Developing CCA methods and procedures
Internal operations and performance	
Service realization process	Cycle time
Law	Effectiveness of legal processes
Regulatory	Government (federal, state, local) relations
Associate related	Leadership, diversity, morale, performance, training
Supplier performance	
Access billing and collections	Contracts and agreements with local exchange carriers, performance quality of billing and collections
Cost and financial	
Market share	Profitability and shareholder value,
Revenue per minute growth	strategic planning, and productivity
Competitive analogs	

Source: Reprinted with permission of AT&T Consumer Communications Services, 1994.

at six sigma it is difficult to avoid shipping defective products. For example, if a company produces the same product of 10,000 parts or processes, at six sigma it will have a defect rate of more than 3 percent; in fact, for every 10,000 units it produces there will be 337 defects. If the company manages to catch 95 percent of these errors before shipment, there will still be seventeen defective products going out the door. While critics accept these statistics as accurate, they still argue that quality improvement pays for itself only up to a point, after which the costs are greater than the benefits. Again, the quality assurance person at Motorola rejects this argument:

> Motorola's experience demonstrates that the higher the quality (or fewer the defects), the lower the costs of prevention and appraisal, as well as failure costs. Each time Motorola has improved quality, the manufacturing cost per unit has declined. There may come a time when we debate the cost of eliminating that last defect, but that does not appear to be in the foreseeable future.
>
> Any company adopting a strategy that sets a level of quality beyond which it will no longer invest for further improvements is establishing a strategy that will ultimately result in the feeling that "our quality is good enough." The logical progression is to declare that "we're no worse than anybody else." Neither of these mind-sets will win the global marketplace.

CI involves more than just common logic. It requires careful analysis of data and the willingness to think outside the box. The quality paradigm has changed sharply over the past decade, and old thinking no longer gets the job done. The Baldrige Award winners are ample proof of that.

Examining Your Own Organizational Performance

Is your organization continuing to innovate its work processes and procedures? Does it have a well-formulated plan of action, ensuring that it is benchmarking the most important processes and procedures, and has it targeted the right organizations for these efforts? Is your enterprise continually striving for continuous improvement? And has it identified and rejected the idea that "when quality is good enough, further improvements are not necessary"? In answering these questions, respond to the following assignments, and ask other members of your management team to do the same.

Assignment 1:

1. What new innovative products, services, or processes has your company introduced in the past twenty-four months? Identify three of the major ones.

   a. _____

   b. _____

   c. _____

2. How successful have these innovations been? On what basis are you making this judgment?

   _____

   _____

   _____

   _____

   _____

   _____

Assignment 2

1. Have you developed a formal benchmarking process? What are the key steps in this process? How are they similar to those used by organizations with whom you partner in these efforts? How are they different?

_____

_____

_____

_____

_____

2. What types of benchmarking do you do—internal, competitive, functional, or generic? What amount of overall improvement is accounted for by each? How do you know?

_____

_____

_____

_____

_____

3. Have you identified pillars and metrics for evaluating your benchmarking and CI efforts? What have you learned as a result of these activities?

_____

_____

_____

_____

_____

4. What do you plan to do over the next twenty-four months to improve your benchmarking and CI efforts? Is there a formal system in place for ensuring that these changes take place?

_____

_____

_____

_____

_____

_____

Assignment 3: On a scale of 1 (do not believe) to 10 (believe strongly), rate your organization's current operating philosophy for the following statements:

Quality is the job
of the quality   Quality is
control department   everyone's job
  1   2   3   4   5   6   7   8   9   10

Training doesn't   Training costs
cost; it saves   a great deal
cost   of money
 10   9   8   7   6   5   4   3   2   1

                          The best quality
New quality   programs do not
programs have high   have high initial
initial costs   costs
  1   2   3   4   5   6   7   8   9   10

As quality goes   Better quality
up, cost actually   actually costs a
comes down   lot of money
 10   9   8   7   6   5   4   3   2   1

Measurement of   All relevant data
data should be kept   should be
to a minimum   collected
  1   2   3   4   5   6   7   8   9   10

"Perfection" should be vigorously pursued								Mistakes will happen; it's human nature	
10	9	8	7	6	5	4	3	2	1

Major mistakes should be prevented and minor ones minimized								All defects, large and small, should be eliminated	
1	2	3	4	5	6	7	8	9	10

In improving quality, large and small gains are necessary								Quality gains come from small, continuous steps	
10	9	8	7	6	5	4	3	2	1

Quality improvement takes a lot of time								Quality doesn't take time; it saves time	
1	2	3	4	5	6	7	8	9	10

Thoughtful speed can improve quality								Speed creates more problems than it solves	
10	9	8	7	6	5	4	3	2	1

Instructions: Total all ten of your response scores, and compare your score to this interpretation key:

Interpretation Key

90–100 points: Your organization is on the cutting edge of quality understanding.

70–90 points: Your organization has not fully accepted some of the truths about quality and has some mistaken beliefs that need to be examined.

<70 points: Your organization needs to review its philosophy and operating data and work to dispel the myths that currently cloud its thinking regarding quality performance.

You probably recognized the self-feedback exercise as the same one that you took in Chapter 1. The purpose of repeating it here is to see if there is now any difference in your thinking and that of your management team since you began reading this book. Compare your scores to your earlier results, and decide whether your thinking regarding the nature and purpose of quality has changed. Have your associates do the same, and then evaluate the results.

Epilogue

Each chapter of this book focused on lessons that were learned from some of America's most successful businesses. Some of these lessons are fairly simple to implement; others require a great deal of effort, because they call for a rethinking of strategy and/or introduction of key changes that will alter the current organizational culture. In all cases, however, these twenty lessons are critical to quality and high performance. Here they are in the same order in which they appeared in the book.

Mind-Sets and Cultural Lessons

Lesson 1: Old myths have to be replaced by new truths.
Lesson 2: Customer value added is the name of the game.
Lesson 3: Training is the paradigm buster.
Lesson 4: Cultural change has to begin with a careful formulation of strategic intent.
Lesson 5: Cultural change will be sustained only if there are adequate support mechanisms.
Lesson 6: Cultural changes have to be validated through measurement.

Operational Lessons

Lesson 1: Identify the key factors that are critical for customer satisfaction.
Lesson 2: Carefully craft forms of feedback for determining customer satisfaction.
Lesson 3: Determine the status of the results and take any necessary action for correcting errors and improving customer satisfaction.
Lesson 4: Make training and development mandatory and ongoing.

Lesson 5:   Develop specific tools that work for the organi-
             zation.
Lesson 6:   Review and measure the value of the training
             tools.
Lesson 7:   Decide what should be tracked.
Lesson 8:   Systematically gather and evaluate the data.
Lesson 9:   Carefully and thoroughly assess personnel per-
             formance.
Lesson 10:   Create a process for fully developing the poten-
             tial of each individual.
Lesson 11:   Develop a system for recognizing all outstand-
             ing performance.
Lesson 12:   Create a reward program that is designed espe-
             cially for your organization.
Lesson 13:   Look for ways to innovate the current work
             processes and procedures.
Lesson 14:   Develop an effective benchmarking and contin-
             uous improvement system that relies on New-
             Age thinking.

Index